INDIAN ADMINISTRATION

INDIAN ADMINISTRATION

LETTERS TO A MEMBER OF PARLIAMENT ON THE INDIAN PROBLEM AND ITS POSSIBLE SOLUTION

HENRY GEORGE KEENE

GYAN

Published by

GYAN

Gyan Publishing House
5, Ansari Road
Daryaganj, New Delhi-110002
Phone: 011-47034999, 9811692060
E-mail: books@gyanbooks.com

Distribution Network
gyanbooks.com
India, USA, Canada, UK, Australia

ISBN: 978-93-7169-022-5 (PB)

First Published, 1867

2nd Impression 2025

Printed at: Gyan Press, Delhi.

INDIAN ADMINISTRATION
Author: HENRY GEORGE KEENE

INDIAN ADMINISTRATION.

LETTERS

TO

A MEMBER OF PARLIAMENT

ON THE

INDIAN PROBLEM

AND

ITS POSSIBLE SOLUTION.

BY

H. G. KEENE,

AUTHOR OF "THE MOGHUL EMPIRE."

"Render to Cæsar the things that are Cæsar's."

1867.

ADVERTISEMENT.

In submitting this little Essay to the judgment of English readers, the writer would wish to guard himself against any objections that may be made against its limited scope. As explained in the concluding letter, it is not his intention to offer these pages as a complete picture of Indian Administration. He merely wishes to point out what he believes to be an evil arising from an insufficient distribution of authority between the Home Government and the Local. In so doing, he has selected a few instances, within his own observation, of mischiefs or shortcomings, real and potential, which are attributable to that cause.

But besides the doctrinarian sentimentalism, which appears to him a danger to be apprehended from a too direct influence of English opinion and action upon a peculiar people like the Natives of India, there is also another danger, at which he has but slightly glanced, arising from "that perpetual want of pence that vexes public men." Not only does India pay a yearly tribute of nearly six millions annually to England, but it is possible that she may come to be regarded as a milch-cow from which more might yet be extracted. And, on the other hand, the supply of men, which her defence is constantly draining from the English labour-market, is beginning to be more and more grudged by the public, however liberally it may be paid for in money. The article on Kaye's Sepoy War, in the *Edinburgh Review* for October, 1866, gives an intelligent expression to this feeling; and it is one that may yet imperil the power of Britain in the East.

The arguments of the Reviewer as to the comparative insignificance of danger from the civil population of India, docile and on the whole well governed, as compared to the standing menace of a large Native Army, cannot be denied by any experienced person. At the same time, it is not so obvious how the Native Army is to be further reduced (it is now less than half what it was before the mutiny, and has no guns,) so as to admit of a large and permanent reduction of the British garrison by which it is at present overawed and kept to its duty. The Police of India, only possessed of a rudimental drill, and having only a small fraction of the force armed with old-fashioned firelocks, appear to fall between two stools; while failing, as noticed in these letters, in the detective branch of their work, they are not, as at present organised, adequate to the domestic and foreign duties of a Native Army.

The remedy would appear to be the localization of the Native Army in times of peace, while it should be mobilized to its extremest capacity in times of war. It is absurd to give the misnomer of Bengal Army to the large force of Sepoys between Prome and Peshawur; but local battalions capable of being sent anywhere in time of need, with a Militia reserve, and enregimented according to tribes as well according to districts, would seem the best method of meeting the difficulty.

One word more as to the satisfaction of the people. Believing that the Indian subjects of the British Crown have, allowing for ignorance, a general tendency to be contented, we must surely deprecate rash interference with the religious habits and institutions of the various denominations into which the natives are divided. Another was a respect for their tenures and laws of property. Of course there were occasions upon which no Government professing civilized principles could abstain from interference in both directions. Such occasions were, the abolition of Suttee (with the corollary removal of legal obstructions to the re-marriage of Hindoo widows); and, in the case of property, the resumption of usurped holdings of land free of revenue demand.

But to go farther in these directions might be very unsafe. It may be better in theory, on the one hand, that the Hindoos and Mussulmans should be converted to Christianity; on the other, it may be better political economy, that all the land should be massed in large holdings and descend, undivided, to the eldest son. But these are not the institutions of the country, and no local Government would attempt to introduce them unless really demanded by the native public.

It is this distinction between endemic and epidemic civilization which the following Letters are intended to enforce. All their faults and deficiencies will be pardoned by the reader who sympathizes with the feeling of the writer on this point. No Austrian General ever lost a campaign, through the necessity of following the orders issued daily for his behoof from Vienna, with more certainty than the local Government would lose India (*absit omen!*) if directed at every step by a distant and practically irresponsible Aulic council.

LETTERS

TO

A MEMBER OF PARLIAMENT

ON THE

INDIAN PROBLEM AND ITS POSSIBLE SOLUTION.

INTRODUCTION.

MY DEAR ———

IN attempting to supply you with some of the information on Indian matters, for which you asked me in a recent letter, I must premise one or two points. You must be prepared for much that will appear dull. A subject cannot be exhausted without some danger of exhaustion to the person to whose attention it is submitted. You will also find me crotchetty at times; this is likewise unavoidable, if I am to give you my own experience and to steer clear of commonplace. Lastly, my treatment will often seem partial, if I am to avoid matters of which I know no more than any one else, and to dwell exclusively on topics and scenes with which I have been long familiar. Fortunately these are amongst the subjects which you most desire to hear of.

The country of Hindoostan Proper was the fountain of the changes which form the new starting point in Indian history, and it is there that their effects were most directly seen. The country that lies between the Sutlej on the north-west and the Soane on the south-east is the home of the races who formed our largest Native Army; and it is the same tract which long ago formed the seat of the ancient Indian empires—it was the source of the Hindoostanee language (now overspreading the whole Peninsula;) the scene of the outbreak of 1857, and of the campaigns by which the sepoys and their sympathizers were subjugated in the following year. As it happens also to be that portion of India of which the writer of these pages has had the longest and closest experience, it would in any case have formed the chief subject of his remarks; but it is hoped that the reasons above recorded will reconcile you to the prominence which you will find assigned to it in what will follow. The great ports of Bombay and Calcutta will always be the points of contact for India with the far east on one side, and with Europe on the other; but the commerce of which they form the *entrepôts* will largely depend upon the degree of success with which the Peninsula is administered in its widest area, where the climate, with the soil and the races it supports, are the finest and most vigorous.

On the 1st of September, 1858, Her Majesty formally assumed the direct sovereignty of the fallen house of Timoor the Lame, which had been long administered by the directors of a mercantile community. Thus much we all know; thus much children of eight years old are learning from their last edition of "Pinnock." What was the real meaning of that change, and how it has affected India and England, are questions which I now invite you to consider.

The distribution of the subject which I propose may seem arbitrary; but some privilege will no doubt be conceded to an author. The first point which seems to require a clear statement, in order that the rest may be intelligibly put, is the political result at home. Did the removal of the Court of Directors, while bringing the Parliamentary Minister nearer to his work—as it undoubtedly did—than when he was called President of the Board of Control, at the same time bring him into closer connection with the people of England, his ultimate constituents; and if so, are they prepared to discharge their duty by seeing that the Secretary does his? Because this is really an all-important preliminary, the people of England have voluntarily assumed the reins of the Indian empire, and it is their bounden duty towards the Father of all mankind to take all possible precautions to see that the Indian empire is worthily conducted.

Our next point will be to inquire similarly how affairs in India were affected by the change; what was the real character of the local administration and of the events which broke it down; and what was the nature of the measures taken on the spot to restore that administration or create another. It will be remembered that the change of *régime* was well received at first in India: but that all enthusiasm was promptly checked and chilled by the consequences of the first direct connection with the Imperial Government. Some peculiarities in Lord Canning's character and conduct will be shown to be connected with this, and a sketch will be finally offered of the state of things to which Sir John Lawrence succeeded.

The ground being thus prepared, I shall next attempt to show the nature of the present situation, dividing it into foreign, home, and financial, and the power and duties of the Governor-General. If I should succeed in showing that this great officer of state has not authority quite commensurate with the extremely tangible nature of his responsibility, it may pave the way to the introduction of my exposition of the theory of empire as I understand it, and for illustrations of the benefit which India and England's connection with India might fairly expect from its adoption.

In performing this task, I am aware that I expose myself to two objections, on account of both of which I must beg for the utmost indulgence. In the first place, I write in remote solitude, where works of reference are hardly to be obtained. And, indeed, it may be said generally, that there is a great deficiency of statistical information on Indian subjects. No Porter has arisen amongst us to chronicle the progress of the nation, and the annual reports issued by the various governments are not compiled upon any uniform plan. It would be wrong not to acknowledge the value of Mr. Waterfield's annual statements, that for 1864-65, just received in India especially; but we want the same thing for *long* periods and with more "comparative statements."

But still more than an absence of statistics, the absence from them of what are called "distinct views," will be injurious to the success of my arguments. Almost every one who writes on politics belongs to a party and is the advocate of some recognised system. This plan divides his readers into two camps—some adopt him as a friend, others accept him as an antagonist. Of myself,—if it be not considered presumptuous to borrow the description given of himself by such a man—I would say, in the words of Coleridge, that I have "to make or find my way a detached individual, *terræ filius*, who is to ask love or service of no one on any more specific relation than that of being a man, and as such to take my chance for the free charities of humanity."

LETTER I.

OF THE SECRETARY OF STATE IN COUNCIL.

IT is not perhaps necessary to give a minute description of the several systems of administration that prevailed in London as to Indian affairs from time to time before the Mutiny, nor even of that which was in force when that event occurred; those systems, especially the last, are fully described in books generally accessible, and have, moreover, so entirely passed away, that you could no more bring people to wish for their restoration than you could get them to want back the heptarchy. Yet there are a few particulars in the old constitution which seem to have had the germs of what still exists, whether good or bad, and it is to those principally that I here propose to draw attention.

By the 33rd Geo. III., ch. 32, the Board of

Control was vested with authority to scrutinise and regulate the affairs of the East India Company. They were to have access to all records necessary for that purpose, and despatches were to be submitted for their revision before being sent to India: these they could require the secret committee, which was the Company's actual executive, to alter; and on the failure of that body to comply with the dictation of the Board, the latter were at liberty to issue their own despatches. Mr. Kaye, from whose work (*Administration of the East India Company*, London, 1853) I have extracted these particulars, further remarks: "This unlimited power of correction is in effect coextensive with the power of initiation; and it would be easy to name cases in which despatches relating to matters of internal administration have lost, under the hands of the minister, all trace of their original significance, and have been made to convey sentiments the very opposite to those entertained by the members of the Court" (of Directors.)

The Secret Committee, above referred to, was composed of the Chairman, Deputy Chairman, and Senior Director; but they could be overridden in the way that we have seen. Doubtless Mr. Kaye, writing as an India House advocate, at a time when the great Company was on its trial, somewhat exaggerated the practical disadvantages of this scheme. He is no doubt right as a historian, and adroit as a partisan when he fastens upon the cry, then so prevalent, of "double government," and turns it to his own profit by saying of the scheme that it obscured responsibility and deluded public opinion. It did so, though not to the utmost possible extent. The President was always ignorant, often indifferent; and it is probable that he willingly left the ordinary administration of affairs in the hands of his experienced and interested colleagues. The instances in which the Board of Control is known to have exercised a direct sway in opposition to the views of the Court are but few, and usually involved imperial questions, upon which the President, and the Cabinet of which he was a member, were liable to be called to account by Parliament. Even the Afghan War, so often made a battle-horse by the extreme opponents of imperialism, was really as much initiated by Indian statesmen as by Sir John Hobhouse; and in the recall of Lord Ellenborough, (whatever judgment we may pass on its propriety,) we must see that the Court of Directors gave a splendid and daring instance of their ready disposition to act up to their full responsibility when they were able to do so.

Nevertheless, the scheme was faulty. Undoubtedly, it had its advantages. The phantom Secretaries flitted on and off the stage, often before they had time to learn the A, B, C of their duty. The old Indians went down to their dingy palace in Leadenhall Street in the meanwhile, and day by day wove the web which they hoped—often with good grounds—to keep from meddling hands. I have above called the Directors "interested:" I used the word in its best sense. There was hardly a man amongst them who had not some close connection with the east. Some had been civil servants, and had exercised proconsular sway over districts as large and as populous as European kingdoms; others had led armies, which had reproduced the heroism of Xenophon and Alexander; here was a retired diplomatist, who had held his life in his hand for years as Britain's representative at a barbarous court, where he had only courage, and honesty, and the prestige of his country's victories, to sustain him in almost hopeless struggles against chicane and sordid selfishness, to which the basest backstairs of Europe afford no rival; and last, but not least, must be remembered the merchant princes, who had led the forlorn hope of commerce into the lands of old romance, and had come back with the peacefully won spoils of "Ternate and Tidore" of "Ormuz and of Ind." To such men, India, the great stand-point in the east of British influence, was justly dear; it was the land of their own youthful labours; and they willingly sent the best scions of their own houses to renew those labours in the desolation of its jungles and the deadly miasma of its sea-ports: their constant connection with the country thus maintained, making them a perpetual representation of its best intelligence and highest interests.

Still, for all that, government is not a matter entirely of sentiment, or even of idea, though the total ignoring of those elements often leads to great disasters. And, however keen the intellligence, however warm the sympathy which the Directors brought to bear upon their work, it was not a seemly spectacle, this kind of doing good by stealth—this administrative blockade-running, by which the body ostensibly responsible to the nation had to try and smuggle their measures past the scrutiny of a minister who might be the puppet of clerks or of his own crotchets. Parliament—always bored with uninteresting duties—was provided with a very decent excuse for neglecting India, by the existence, and by the usually smooth working of the Court of Directors. But, in the autumn of 1858, when the suppression of the Sepoy revolt was virtually accomplished, this system was utterly abolished. The Sepoys had succeeded to the ear, however disappointed as to the sense. They had risen on the centenary of Plassey, to put down the *raj* of the Company; it was to be now seen what they had got in its place. In August an Act received the Royal assent (21st and 22nd Vic., c. 106) "for the better Government of India," by which it was provided that all powers and rights vested in the East India Company, in trust for Her Majesty, should cease, and should become vested in Her Majesty, and be exercised in her name; and in the following November, a proclamation was solemnly promulgated in this country, in which Queen Victoria was made to claim allegiance of its princes and peoples, under the style and title of "Queen of the United

Kingdom of Great Britain and Ireland, and of the colonies and dependencies thereof in Europe, Asia, America and Australasia" (the Cape and other African colonies not being apparently thought of.)

Such was the decorative (or what we may call the "Heralds' College") view of the transaction. But practically it took, of course, a very different shape. The Court of Directors being put into the political crucible, yielded a precipitate, in the form of fifteen gentlemen, who were to form a council for deliberative purposes; while the President of the Board rose like a phœnix from the conflagration, under the description of "Secretary of State for India." The members of this council were not allowed to be also members of Parliament, nor to vote at a meeting where less than five were present; and they were to have no executive power, except a *veto* in matters purely of a financial character.

Here, then, seems the model we had so long sought. Indian sympathy and experience still sit at the elbow of the minister, but he alone is responsible to parliament; only the question still remains as to practice.

Does Parliament do its duty in the matter?

Are the old Indians allowed to do theirs? Is the minister really controlled by the imperial legislature; and is he really benefited by the advice of his own council? or is he liable to the fate of the proverbial sitter upon two stools, sometimes made to sacrifice his obscure and uninteresting charge, when the policy of the cabinet requires it, and on all other occasions subject to the temptation to send out to India ignorant, injudicious and vexatious orders about matters of local administration, which he had better leave alone?

LETTER II.

OF THE CHANGE AS FELT IN INDIA, AND OF THE LOCAL RECONSTRUCTION.

ANGLO-INDIANS are sceptical, and as such they are naturally credulous. When we first heard that the crown and senate of England had withdrawn their auspice from the East India Company and entered upon the direct management of this country, there was no limit to the expectations in which we allowed ourselves to indulge. This feeling was by no means confined to those who, from their peculiar mental habits, had always refused to take optimist views of the Honourable Court's administration. If we were to judge from the local journalism of that day, all grievances were not only to be at once redressed, but to be rendered impossible for the future; and a millennium was at hand, when the planter should lie down with the ryot, and the competition-wallah should lead them. We all caught the fever of loyalty; lighted all our spare tallow-candles and oil-*lamps*, and threw up hats, caps, helmets and *turbans* in honour of what, in our enthusiasm, we called "the accession of Victoria, the beloved Empress of Hindoostan."

Alas, alas! the scene soon changed. The lights are fled, the hats worn out, the halls of bunkum resound no more with loyal outcries.

The first sign of the reaction arose in the army, where it has continued to rage chronically ever since. I may, therefore, be pardoned if I offer a few remarks upon the former position of the officers, with especial reference to the native Bengal army, the mutiny of which had been the immediate cause of the changes under discussion. It is important to do this, not only on account of the unprecedented height to which the discontents of those officers have since risen (within lawful limits, that is), and the extraordinary length of time for which they have lasted, but also on account of the opinion which has been here and there expressed, that these officers had been mainly answerable for the outbreak of the native troops. Even before the mutiny, a British officer of rank, who had seen service with the Bengal army, said, that owing to the principle of staff employ that prevailed, the regimental officers were the "refuse" of the list; while a well-known Bombay reformer had not scrupled to support the statement by very analogous language.

Now, I will not say that the system on which Sepoy corps were officered had nothing to do with the relaxation of discipline, which largely lubricated the progress of disaffection; but I will undertake to prove that, barring human fallibility, there was no peculiar blame attaching to the officers themselves. I will also beg attention to a few words upon some of the real reasons which had prepared and precipitated this terrible revolt of 100,000 trained soldiers.

I venture to think that the discussions in Mr. Kaye's book (*Sepoy War*, Vol. I., p. 324), though full of interest, are not necessary to enable us to understand how the Bengal army lost its allegiance. The history of countries like India, in point of civilization, is full of instances of a prætorian spirit, and this is the cause that Sir John Lawrence, with his usual decision, has publicly and repeatedly assigned as the chief one. The destruction of the Strelibzes in Russia, of the Mamelukes in Egypt, of the

Janissaries in Constantinople, are familiar cases in which a despotic government has had to annihilate, in self-preservation, the machine that it had elaborated for the maintenance of its sway. Other cases might be mentioned in which such a machine has proved too strong to be destroyed, and then it has been the government itself which has fallen, like a magician torn to pieces by the powers he had raised from earth or air. But it is more comforting for the friends of order and of progress to dwell on instances which show that a government in whose plans these elements in any degree preponderate, is sure to be the conqueror at last, however dear may be its victory, and whatever suffering may, for the time, appear to cloud its triumph. Now, the Sepoy was a good servant; he had stood by his leaders in moments of great trial; he had aided them to conquer the bravest and the best drilled of his own countrymen, and had perished by their side in the snows of Afghanistan. But he was a bad master. To the pride of caste he had added the pride of soldiership;* he looked upon himself as *homme nécessaire;* he domineered in the bazaars, and swaggered in his village. This

* See Appendix I.

was naturally not distasteful to his officers, as long as the officers themselves were not the victims; and surely it is scarcely a matter of reproach to these gentlemen if the feeling of comradeship had surmounted the barriers of race, and they took a pride in their tall, showy followers, and treated them as friends. Indeed, it would not be difficult to bring forward instances which would seem to show that the officers who fared the worst in the mutiny were often among those who had shown the greatest regard for their men.

But, if it was an unavoidable touch of human weakness that the officers should be thus prejudiced, yet it is probable that the feeling would have produced good rather than evil, if they had only been trusted by the authorities, and given full powers by which to curb the exuberant *outrecuidance* of their men. Unhappily, a long course of Whig interference had entirely sapped the jurisdiction of all local functionaries, civil and military alike. The Asiatic, strange as it may sound, walks by sight rather than by faith; and treats his king as the frogs did theirs, when he finds him but a log. A reference to the Acts and Orders of the Indian Government for the period during which the last charter lasted, will show to what an extent "Liberal" principles had led up to centralization. Take for example the abandonment of the grant of "Half Batta," which undoubtedly lowered the regimental officers in the eyes of their men; the prohibition to flog Sepoys, though European soldiers, remained subject to the last; and the gradual withdrawal of powers from captains of companies and from regimental courts martial, about and since the framing of the Reform Bill.

Now it will be fair to admit, once for all, that the Sepoys had grievances. Their pay and allowances had been tampered with; their promotion and superannuation were both in an unsatisfactory state; and, under Lord Dalhousie's iron rule, they were treated with a coldness which, though more to be commended than the extreme of indulgence, only succeeds with uneducated men, when they see the visible symbols of force in your hand. For example, in 1853-54, the Governor-General permitted a regiment of horse (the 8th Irregulars) to volunteer for Burmah, where a number of men lost their lives, and many more lost their horses—their own property in these corps. The men bore the punishment and damage silently for the period of their covenant—two full years—and because they declined to renew it, were made the subjects of one of those stinging orders which his Lordship so well knew how to write. Then, because the feelings and prejudices of Sepoys were found to be opposed to being sent on foreign service, it was decreed that all regiments should, in future, be enlisted for "general service," a great blow to men who had been in the habit of bringing forward their brothers and sons to take their place in what had hitherto, in most instances, been merely a sort of mobilised militia. It must be remembered that these men were only mercenaries after all, they were not fighting for patriotism, but for pay and social privileges; and when these were threatened, they were ready to rise on their own account, or to become the tools of any discontented persons who could make it seem worth their while to transfer to themselves their allegiance.

And it cannot be denied that the *system* of regimental management had its share in creating these grievances and in fostering the spirit in which they were resented. And it may be further admitted that, when the revolt had been suppressed, many of the reforms that ensued were of a salutary character, though the best were not of home manufacture. These last may be thus briefly described:—Officers holding staff employ were to be attracted by a step of rank at the same time that they were allowed to go on rising in their regiments into a staff corps from whence were to be provided the new leaders for the new Native Army organised on a partly irregular plan. But as this plan required far fewer officers than before, there would be a large balance of officers left without employment. Of these the seniors were to be bought out; and those who remained to form, along with their favoured brethren of the staff corps, cadres bearing the numbers of the old disbanded regiments, to be paid for doing nothing, and allowed to absorb by retirement or death. Now, not merely was this a degrading prospect for men who had any spark of military spirit, and who were conscious of having hitherto done their duty, but it was an actual punishment in the loss of promotion and in the supercession in army rank and pay, which was a result of the formation of the staff corps. These grievances have been so long before the world, and are so amply set forth by the Officers' Committee (*vide* their

Observations, fol. pp. 198,) that it is not necessary for me to spoil the proportions of this little essay by entering into details. They may be briefly summed up in these words:—Officers entering the Staff Corps continued to encumber the regimental cadres: there were nearly 6,000 European officers in the Company's Army, of which upwards of 4,000 were attached to Native Corps. About 1,300 went into the Staff Corps; the rest were ruined. All, however, has now (September, 1866) been happily redressed, as it would have been some years ago if left to the local Government.

This much, however, it was proper to say in order that it might be understood what was the first instance of the working of the direct Government with which the public in India became generally acquainted. It was not calculated to feed their loyalty. I shall proceed to notice a few other matters which combined still further to chill the enthusiasm with which we had at first welcomed the new *régime*.

Still more ill-omened was the manner in which the late Company's European troops received the change. At first, it took them by surprise, but it was not long before they found out that their transfer could not be effected without their own consent; and that if they took service under the Crown, it must be by way of voluntary enlistment. They, therefore, demanded a bounty, and this being refused, 12,000 men took their discharge, and obtained a free passage to England. Lord Canning then, of his own authority, conceded the bounty, and the remainder of the men stayed peacefully in India, where their services were secured for a comparatively small outlay.

It has been above hinted, that the measures which paved the way to the great Mutiny had been taken by orders of the Home Government at a time when the "man-and-brother" theory was so prevalent in England; and we have now seen a fair example of a home measure—the Amalgamation—producing a great military discontent, ere the ashes of that Mutiny had been well stamped cold. I shall proceed to give a few instances of a similar interference in Civil matters, producing similar results.

Lord Canning, who had been very unpopular on account of his cool composure and somewhat frigid justice during the Mutiny and its suppression, wished, apparently, to conciliate the European community towards the end of his reign.

Accordingly, just as he was leaving India, he issued orders for the sale of Crown lands and the redemption of the Government dues on other estates. In a few months the Secretary of State sent out an order peremptorily cancelling Lord Canning's, and substituting measures of his own. Some of the consequences were ludicrous, some sad. People who had only paid money could get it back again; but what was the position of a man who had sunk time, health, and capital in reclaiming malarious tracts of forest on the faith of a Viceroy, and then had to see them all lost by the *fiat* of a remote Minister? Similar cases occurred with regard to Taxation; an English Financier was sent out to impose upon the people of India, Native and European, a tax which seemed so dangerous, that a Governer of Madras hazarded his appointment sooner than let it pass without protest, and which succeeded in drawing at the rate of about three half-pence a head on an average of the whole population, after subjecting them to trouble, and a scrutiny into private affairs, and a demoralisation that cannot be estimated. On the capitalisation of Land Revenue, and on the amount of import duties, a similar conflict of jurisdiction took place between the Governments, home and local; so that it became a point publicly raised by a Member of Parliament who had once held office in Calcutta, as to what was the province of each.

Now, whatever opinion individuals may form for themselves about each particular measure, thinking according to various circumstances, that here the Secretary was right, and there the Viceroy, surely the last statement should shock all alike,—that a man in Mr. Laing's position should not be able to pronounce positively as to the respective province of each. One would have thought that, in the department over which he had presided when in India, there would be less doubt than usual. When one considers the immense peculiarity of Eastern Finance, its almost total independence of direct taxation—the enormous net balance India yields to England, amounting for 1866-67 to more than five and a quarter millions (*vide* note at end of letter)—and the refusal of Parliament to pledge British credit for Indian loans, one would think that this was a matter, if any was, for the unfettered action of the Local Government; yet we see that this is not the fact. Not only is the

Indian Government unable to raise loans at the market rate for want of an imperial guarantee; but we have lately seen a most important line of railway—the proposed extension from Lahore to the frontier—checked because the Chancellor of the Exchequer thought it unadvisable, in the existing state of commerce, that India should get money from England at any price whatever. Finally, we were not allowed to coin gold for our own use, and an arbitrary rate of exchange unfairly hostile to us is still imposed by the Home Government on transactions between the two countries.

India is a conquered country, and must pay whatever the mother country pleases to exact. But in a paper devoted to a consideration of the popularity of the existing form of Government, it is surely not out of place to notice a few of the causes which appear to be operating with an increasing force to dissatisfy public opinion in this country. That opinion is at present vaguely and weakly expressed, and it is self-contradictory upon many points of detail; the feelings and desires of the natives—even when well informed—being different from, and sometimes opposed to, those of the European settlers.

But I have written in the interests of the whole country, not in those of any class; and I believe that class interests have a natural tendency to reconciliation, unless fostered by ignorant interference.

NOTE.—Appended to Mr. Massey's Budget the printed accounts of India for 1866-67 show that while the revenues realised are forty-six and three quarter millions, the expenditure was estimated at only forty-one and one quarter; nearly twelve per cent. to the good! But on the other hand, close upon eight millions go to England as payment on account of interest on stock and on railway shares, and to pay for military and civil charges, for more than five of which she gets no return, and of which more than two and a quarter millions have to be taken from the cash balances, *i.e.*, from reserved capital. So that though unprecedentedly solvent, India is subject to a hæmorrhage that will be fatal if not arrested.

LETTER III.

OF THE SAME IN REGARD TO (SO-CALLED) FOREIGN AFFAIRS.

NEXT among the questions we have proposed for discussion comes that of the relation of the present British Government to the native States—what is, in the technical phrase of Anglo-Indian administration, called "the Political Department," and there are few questions more obviously ripe for treatment of a scientific sort. The popular view is that all the "country powers" (to use a sensible old phrase of the last century) are independent sovereigns, overshadowed, threatened, and often destroyed by the crimson glare of British conquest; and although we have had little serious talk of *restitution*, yet there is no doubt a disposition in England to perform minor acts of penance in periods of national despondency. Thus, in 1857, though no one publicly proposed, as far as I am aware, that the Punjab should be made over to the Maharajah Dhuleep Singh, yet there was a pretty general confession that "the policy of annexation" was very wrong, and that Lord Dalhousie, or somebody,—it was not quite clear who,—had been greatly to blame. Now, let us take this same Punjab as a crucial instance of annexation, and we shall find it to combine almost all the singular anomalies that beset the subject. At the end of the last century there were a number of Jat leaders—a kind of glorified *Jacquerie*—who had, in the decay of the Moghul Empire, overthrown the hereditary nobles and got into a kind of baronial position of their own: secure in mud and forts, and the following of a bold and not very scrupulous peasantry, they defied the Viceroys in their own country, and often carried desolation to the very glacis of the Delhi fortifications. After the Empire had fallen, Runjeet Singh, a Punjab leader, more astute than his neighbours, made a treaty with the British envoy in 1809, by which he cemented a friendship which lasted for the rest of his long life between "the British Government and the State of Lahore;" yet at that time the young envoy thus described the

Rajah:—"During the time of the Mahrattas his power was very petty, compared with what it is at present. He had not then subdued many chiefs of the Punjab, and would not presume to extend his views beyond the Sutlej. As late as 1803 . . . he was not the sovereign of places in the Punjab within thirty miles of Lahore." (*Mr. Metcalfe to Government, June* 2, 1803—see *Life of Lord Metcalfe*, p. 242.) But in 1803 the Mahrattas were expelled from Delhi by the British; so that we may fairly say, that when he ultimately became ruler of the Punjab, Runjeet Singh was as such our creature. The same may be said of a great many other native States, of the origin of most of these powers, and of our connection with them. An account will be found in Campbell's *Modern India* (Chap. IV.), where it is stated that, as a rule, none of them date earlier than 1720. And as the Emperor Furokhseer had, some years earlier than that date, received a British embassy and sanctioned the Company's establishment at the mouths of the Hooghly, it may be said that we are an older power in India than most of the native States. So that at first sight it might be thought, that not only is the popular view wrong, but that India has, in fact, been the subject of a scramble in which the strongest was at liberty to clothe himself with any rights he could get hold of. On looking, indeed, into the list of native powers as they existed in 1720,—or what is more to the purpose, in 1802,—when we first appeared in Hindustan as conquerors, we shall find that there were several States not merely practically independent, but of such long standing that the most ancient houses in Europe are, in comparison, but the gourds of a night. Such were Travancore and Mysore in the south, and such, more notably still, the solar and lunar dynasties of Rajpootana. And not only so, but there was the empire itself, very visible even in its decay, when the daubing of Mahratta usurpation was removed; and this surely, the peacock-throne of Shah Jehan, the iron sceptre of Aurungzebe, had to be acknowledged by conquerors who acknowledged a law of nations.

Now it happens that the political position, which a legal theory would tend to establish, is precisely that which Government, on that occasion, actually did assume. The Peshwa—head of the Mahratta Confederacy—was at that time Plenipotentiary Minister or Viceregent of the Empire, and his mayor of the palace, Dowlut

Rao Scindia, was his deputy. It is plain, therefore, that when we expelled Sindia's army from Hindoostan, and took possession of the palace and person of the Mogul, we simply stepped into the situation of plenipotentiary minister.* Viewed in this light, all that has followed becomes intelligible. Our relations with native powers,—whether they were chief commissioners who had usurped hereditary succession in the decrepitude of the central authority; or barons who, by the favour of the minister, had become possessed of civil jurisdiction; generals, who had turned into principalities the fiefs assigned for the pay of their troops; or heaven-descended Ranas, whose thrones (though always subordinate to some central power) were in existence when Alexander encountered Porus, —all were precisely what those of our predecessor had been. If the empire of Hindustan extended over the Punjab, Rajpootana and the Deccan, then obviously the most powerful chiefs, the most far-descended rulers, were all delegates or feudatories of the imperial Government—of

* "The Maharaja Dowlut Rao Scindiah hereby renounces all claims upon his Majesty Shah Alum, and engages on his part to interfere no further in the affairs of his Majesty." *Treaty of Surja Anjingaum* 30*th December*, 1803.

"us and our king. And when the latter, in 1857, chose to murder the British Resident and take the command of the army, he raised a perfectly plain issue, on which he was defeated, and (as usually happens in such cases) fell. It need only be added to this brief *résume* that the use of the word "feudatory" is in strict accordance with the present position of the intermediate rulers in reference to the imperial power: the nature of feudal tenure, it will be recollected, is a just description of theirs, *viz.*, a holding of land in consideration of service. By a less happy metaphor writers who ought to know better, sometimes speak of the imperial power as the "suzerain," that term being more appropriate to the native powers themselves in relation to their own tenants, while the only feudal title appropriate to that of Britain in the East is the old and easily understood one—"Sovereign."

Should I be here pressed with my reference to the law of nations, and reminded that the Court of Directors, through their agents in India made treaties with the native powers, and that treaties imply equal sovereign rights, I can only answer that, though on the whole I find no trace of conscious violation of the law of nations in the conduct of the Company, yet that we are not to expect in a struggle for empire, that Vattel should be strictly followed in his technical details; and that after all the *principle* was not violated. As Vicegerent of the Moghul Empire, the Governor-General for the time being was only *primus inter pares* with native rulers; and it is very observable that, on the occupation of Delhi by General Lake, Lord Wellesley never entered into any treaty with the fallen Emperor; as if he knew that such a treaty was beyond even his authority. The Emperor of those days and his sons wrote to our George III. on terms of brotherhood, and coin continued to be struck, and public proclamations made, in the name of the titular sovereign for very many years. Down to 1857 our "annexation policy" was merely the same Aaron's rod process, which other suzerain powers had exercised, Shoja-od-Dowlah in Rohilkund, and still later, Runjeet Singh (our original instance *v. sup.*) in the Punjab.

As co-ordinate vassals of the Empire, we made a covenant with the Lahore ruler in 1809; in 1846 we made a fresh arrangement, and even at the annexation, only acted as any powerful minister might have done.

But *after* 1857, when the great *coup d'etat* of Bahadoor Shah had failed, and he was sent to die an exile at Rangoon, there was then only one last annexation left to be made, the wondrous rod had swallowed Pharaoh himself; *only the rod* remained to be disposed of; and that done, we can no more talk of annexation in India than in the British Islands. No one called Pitt's union between Ireland and England an act of annexation; nor would it be an act of annexation, if the Secretary of State were to send out a despatch next month ordering that the Nizam should be pensioned, and his territory made over to a British Commissioner.

This, then, is the "political" change (taking the word in its restricted Indian sense) that has followed upon the suppression of the Mutiny. The great annexers have been themselves annexed; the Emperor of Delhi and his Vicegerent Plenipotentiary have been alike disposed of; the Moghul Empire and the Court of Directors have alike ceased to be; India is become a province of the Empire of Britain. But under such circumstances the position of the native princes is, within certain limits, safer than before. They have ceased to be barbarous barons snatching a temporary immunity for selfish tyranny, or sulkily awaiting the flow of the red tide; they have become mediatized into tenants-in-chief, guided by a common law of good conscience, and moving in conformity with the unity of the Imperial Cosmos.

If these principles be admitted, it will undoubtedly follow that although *cœteris paribus*, all native rules of succession* will be allowed to operate in the transmission of these titles and powers, and the whole force of the Empire if need be, will support the holders of them in all just rights, yet that those holders must be held strictly responsible that they do not habitually abuse their powers or make their rights a source of general wrong. This is, perhaps, as plain an instance as can be found of the respective operations appropriate to the Home and the Local Governments. It is for the Viceroy to see that the country committed to his trust is well administered; but it is still right that the Imperial centre should have a casting voice in the punishment of Imperial officers. Palestine was made into a Roman

* Any one familiar with Mr. Maine's "Ancient Law" will understand this. There is no foundation for any distinction between an ordinary and an adopted Hindoo son.

province by Augustus; but Antipas, Philip and Agrippa, were as much subject to control, and entitled to protection, as Pilate, or Festus, or Felix.

There is one point connected with the punishment of a feudatory, and the protection of his vassals, which might well be commended to the attention of the Imperial Government and the people of the metropolis. Need the removal of an incompetent native tyrant be always the precursor of the introduction into his territories of the British Chief Commissioner, the Settlement Officer, and the Civil Code? Is it a fact that those parts of India are the happiest where all official promotion is reserved for foreigners, and where batches of law reform are constantly supplied, hot and hot, from the central furnace of European civilisation? Railway, telegraphs, canals, penal codes, philosophic systems of jurisprudence, may tend to make a country progressive; but do they always make the inhabitants happy and contented, or may they not sometimes make them partakers in that heritage of woe that is bequeathed to us modern English from centuries of doubt, and discontent, and conflict? Does it not seem cruel to throw over the laughing sky of the East, and over the contented faces of its easy-going inhabitants, the clouds gathered in the cold atmosphere of our egotistic competition? The simple wants, the tribal charities, the patient labours of a primitive people, where the individual is being constantly suppressed, and the social bond kept in a natural slackness by the small size and well-defined character of the groups round which it is thrown; all these must be powerfully affected when the administrative machinery of the West is transplanted full grown to throw its cold shade over the land.

Perhaps I am exaggerating the disadvantages of our civilisation, and the sufferings of alien races when too much pressed upon by it; but there is one way in which, at all events, we might mitigate the suddenness with which relief is apt to be afforded in such cases. When Sir William Sleeman, in 1851, reported upon the mal-administration of Oudh, he mentioned, as one scheme for the reform of the Government of that afflicted country, that it should be entrusted to a Native Board of Administration, with which a British officer should be associated. This scheme had been tried in the Punjab and had failed; and perhaps that is a reason why it was not repeated. But we, judging from the event, are surely entitled to say, that it did not fail worse than the other. When we finally drove the Khalsa army into the Sutlej, and associated Sir F. Currie with the Durbar at Lahore, we may have omitted to attend to something which, though only a point of detail, was essential to the welfare of the measure; and after all, the rising of Moolraj and of Shere Singh was not so deadly in its character, nor so universal in its spread, as the rising of the people of Oudh in 1857. It is the cutting down the tall poppies, the substituting the scrivener's pen and the auctioneer's hammer for the sword and gun, and English stipendiaries for native magnates, and the drying up all legitimate channels of native ambition, which really humiliate a people that we are seeking to raise. However necessary such measures may be in our own provinces, where our own system is irrevocably committed to practice for evil or for good, it is not so certain that they will be attended with success in new territories. Perhaps even Ireland might be cited as a rebuke to an over-weening civiliser.

From what has been said, it will be seen that the common opinion, that "the days of annexation are no more," is true rather in letter than in spirit. You may annex Burmah, Belochistan, or Nepal, but you can now no more annex any territory within Indian limits, than you can the Isle of Man. Yet the very proclamation of 1858, and the words and deeds which have followed it in India, though intended to calm actual anxieties as to the continuation of Lord Dalhousie's policy, involve an assumption from which the great proconsul would have shrunk in his boldest moments. What was formerly the extension of a grasping neighbour, is now the undisguised claim of paramount sovereignty. Nor is this theory alone. The permission to adopt; the threats uttered at Lord Canning's durbars; the honours conferred on Rajah Dinkur Rao, the late enlightened Prime Minister of Sindia; the commendation lately bestowed on the petty Chief of Khetree for improving his administration; and, later still, the placing of Bahawulpore under the Commissioner of Mooltan,—are all instances of sovereign action perfectly legitimate, and capable of being pushed to any length.

There are two ways in which this new substitute for annexation may be exercised, confiscation and sequestration. We shall not often find instances where modern feeling would justify the former, but the placing of a Native State, for a longer or shorter time, under managers selected by the paramount power, is a thing which must sometimes happen; and it is most desirable that all Native Chiefs should know that such possibilities exist. Only let it be borne in mind, that all appearance of *greediness* should be avoided, together with the putting of new wine into old bottles, by suddenly anglicising the whole administration of the absorbed districts, and above all let the Chief thus punished have an appeal to the Parliament of the British Empire. We are fortunate to-day in having a Viceroy of high character, and who knows every detail of his duty; to-morrow we may have a noble gold-stick, who will merely carry out the caprices of a clever but irresponsible "Foreign" Secretary at Simla or Calcutta.

LETTER IV.

IN REGARD TO THE HOME DEPARTMENT—REVENUE.

Great changes, in what is called the Political, or, still more technically, "Foreign," Department of India administration, followed the suppression of the Revolt. Great changes have also taken place in the "Home" Department; but it is not so easy to say how far they are attributable to the Revolution of 1857. The relations of the Viceroy towards Native Chiefs are different *in principle* from those which the Company's Governor-General held towards the "country powers," and the word "Foreign" is no longer applicable; for these "political" purposes, the Great Peninsula has all become "one red." But an observer of the direction which affairs had been taking in the last few years before 1857, will perceive that the Marquis of Dalhousie, in "Home" matters, had already entered upon the very path which is now being pursued. It is too much to say that, had he remained at the helm, the vessel of State would not have run upon the hidden rocks, which so nearly reduced her for a time to a condition of wreck. His eyes were too constantly fixed upon the stars of his magnificent ambition, and he might not have seen the breakers; though, if by any chance, his retirement had not taken place when it did, he would assuredly have carried out many, if not all, the measures of progress which are now working such wonders. Still, to whatever cause attributable, the measures are here; and it will not be out of place to give a brief notice of them, if only to show how much remains yet, which only the local Government can properly effect, and in which minute interference from London has done mischief which should be no more repeated.

The first and most important topic connected with internal affairs, is Revenue, the sinews of war, but the life-blood of the arts of peace. It is in vain for the Imperial Government to urge upon India the extension of public works, whilst it not only draws a nett yearly tribute of nearly £6,000,000* sterling from her, but refuses to pledge its credit to her loans; and interferes not merely with her sea customs (which are indeed matter of Imperial concernment), but also with her management of fiscal and financial affairs, which touch her vitally, and her alone.

It is generally admitted, that Indian revenue has a very weak point. The receipts from opium are annually so large, that there is a constant tendency to reckon upon them; but that tendency has to be as constantly checked. The estimate for the current year was seven and three-quarter millions, while the actual receipts exceeded eight millions and a-half. This gratifying result has accordingly been accepted, as the basis of the estimate for the coming year; but suppose the difference this time to be in the opposite direction. It is easy to see how this may happen. The opium revenue is the last relic of the old trading monopoly of the Court

* I have above shown that the *gross* amount drawn from India this year will be £8,000,000. The "Quarterly Review," to be noticed more fully below, puts the dead loss to India at fully £6,000,000.

of Directors, and thus we may have an item of upwards of 1,000,000 sterling dependent upon the chances of the market. Any one can see that if the Chinese—our main customers—took to growing their own opium, this source of revenue would be greatly affected, as it would also be if the moral conscience of the people of England were to rise and prohibit a system which causes chronic vice amongst our neighbours, with intermittent fits of questionable fighting. But, even setting that apart, the price of opium varies from rs. 75 to rs. 150 per chest, and this margin must always be allowed for.

Hitherto such fluctuations have been more than met by the steady advance of revenue derived from land. This again was a relic of old times, though in a different way from opium, the Indian Government here appearing in the character of landlord, as it formerly did in that of merchant, and gaining from the judicious expenditure of capital a progressive increase. From 1850 to 1860, the increase in this item was about cent. per cent., and the amount now is nearly half of the total revenue of the country, while the charges of collection are barely 10 per cent., or less than half those on the opium.* It seems hardly credible, under these circumstances, that Sir C. Wood, in 1862, should have sent out orders to stagnate this wonderful source of supply, by fixing the demand in perpetuity. Yet since, in spite of the Chancellor Oxenstiern, the rulers of the world are *not* selected on account of folly, it is proper respectfully to consider the arguments on which this policy is based. The despatch referred to, and the minutes of Indian councillors by which it was accompanied, were analysed at the time in *Blackwood's Edinburgh Magazine*, and subsequently in a pamphlet † published in Calcutta. They were briefly these:—

Politically, the landholders would be attached to a rule which secured them fixity of tenure at a fixed rent, and it was this class rather than the peasantry, whom it was our interest to conciliate.

Financially, the development of secondary

* Land Revenue	£20,254,300
Charges	2,058,570
Opium Revenue	8,500,000
Charges	1,762,940

These figures are taken from Mr. Massey's Budget Statement to the Legislative Council. May, 1866.

† *Suggestions on the Land Revenue of India:* by a Collector. Calcutta, G. C. Hay and Co.

wants, which would ultimately ensue, would largely increase the remaining branches of the revenue; any balance being left to be recouped by other methods of taxation.

To this was added a philanthropic argument, founded on the absence of famines in Bengal, where the land revenue was already fixed in perpetuity; such visitations being apt to recur from time to time in parts of India where that system did not exist.

These arguments were all discussed in the papers above referred to, and I must not destroy the proportions of the present essay by repeating the discussion in full. But it may be useful to point out the leading fallacy which runs through each.

No arguments are needed to show that the result of a permanent settlement is to create a landed aristocracy. True you may fix in perpetuity the demand upon peasant proprietors, but the improvidence of the uneducated, and the withdrawal of State capital from agricultural works, the desire of the rich for land, and their weight and influence in corrupt law courts, must undoubtedly combine to effect this result, the avowed object of Lord Cornwallis, and probably the most desirable state of society in the eyes of nine-tenths of English statesmen. It would be unbecoming on the part of the present writer to go out of his province to attack the English system, by which poverty, ignorance, dependence and crime seem rendered certain, and where the luxuries of the landlord allow of the depopulation of extensive districts. It suits the English, and those to whom that is not sufficient answer, can consult the works of Mr. Stuart Mill, M.P., or the opinions of intelligent continental observers, like the Prussian Agriculturist who wrote a paper on the subject in the *Cornhill Magazine* for August, 1866. Well, then, granting that an agricultural aristocracy will be the result of a permanent settlement, is it not mere speculation to say that they will be more loyal than the bulk of the agriculturists now are? I will not press the argument, that Asiatic nature has peculiarities preventing its action being always calculated upon from the rules of human nature at large; but I will ask, why is the permanent Zemindar to feel that no change can ever bene fit him? I maintain that there are two points in our fixed system, which he would get rid of in any Revolution, that overthrow our power, yet which, as long as we sway India, no form of permanent settlement can alter. I mean *payment in cash*, and *sale by auction for default*, than which it would be impossible to name two points more unpopular with those concerned, or more inseparable from our system. Under any native *régime*, whatever its faults might be, a landholder would always be allowed to pay the Government demand *in kind*, and if he fell into arrears, he might be subject to many annoyances, and his land might be sequestrated, but he would be spared the indignity of hearing a hard official putting up to public outcry the acres of his ancestors. Undoubtedly you may create a landed class, but they would, under the influence of this process, in no long time break down, and be replaced by absentee money-dealers ; the thing has happened in Bengal, and there is nothing in the habits of less civilized parts of India to prevent it happening there also. And when these changes have taken place, the old aristocracy will surely have no motive to love our rule, nor their mercantile successors much capacity to support it. The Collector of Jounpoor, one of the few North-West Districts where the permanent settlement has always existed, reported in 1863 that none of the old families retained any land. And this, be it remembered, under a settlement which allowed them to rack-rent their tenantry, and, being based on imperfectly known assets, took from them much less than the State's fair proportion.

But I must hurry on to the financial part of the question. It is not denied, that the loss of revenue will be considerable. It will happen in this way:—Money now has in India about six times the purchasing power that it has in England. The pay of a constable, to take one of the highest sorts of unskilled labour, is three shillings a week, and the wages of a common workman about two. But, as India enters into the markets of the world, this must have a tendency to diminish; and the result of an examination into prices current for many years back, has been to show that the average rate at which the value of money is falling is at least one per cent. per annum. "Since 1852 rates of labour have increased 30 per cent. throughout the whole of India" (*Waterfield's Report*, 1864-65, p. 41,) consequently a time will come, say in fifty years, when the expenses of collection, which are now two millions, will be four, and so of other items of expenditure, till the Land Revenue, now forming nearly half the total income of the State, will only form a quarter. The balance is in the air. "An increase of secondary wants," "other forms of taxation," surely this is windy doctrine to teach us "poor Indians," however untutored be our minds. As soon shall the Ethiop change his skin, as the Hindoo smoke Havannas, or the Moslem eat overland ham; and, as for "other forms of taxation," it seems to have been overlooked that the Land Revenue is no tax at all,* but a division by the State acting as steward, in which the whole contributable body benefits in the surplus produce of the soil, in lieu of its being monopolized by a few selfish landlords. The Eastern may not be so good a plan in the abstract as that which prevails in England, but at all events, it has continued indigenous and familiar here, at least since the time of Strabo. Surely, it is contrary to the maxims of a sound conservatism, to disturb it in favour of a system which is still vehemently denounced in most parts of Europe, nay, by some of the foremost thinkers in England itself.

* "As far as this source goes, the people remain untaxed. The wants of Government are supplied without any drain upon the produce of any man's labour, or of any man's capital."—*Evidence of Mr. James Mill before Parliamentary Committee.*

LETTER V.

THE SAME CONTINUED. THE INCOME TAX, AND FINANCE.

THERE is also urged in favour of a permanent settlement of the land, a well-known philanthropic argument, first introduced, I believe, by the late Colonel Baird Smith. Bengal being the channel of the S.E. monsoon, is not often visited by a failure of the periodical rains. This circumstance led the gallant Colonel to mistake the *post hoc* for the *propter hoc*, and to attribute to the permanent settlement what was due to physical circumstances. In the meantime, the Government of Bengal, not alarmed for the future of their green and fertile Province, and having lost all direct interest in the development of her productive powers, had provided neither roads nor canals, nor any of those public works by which famine is guarded against or alleviated, and which, if not done by Government in India, are not done at all. The contrast, in ordinary times, between the state of the people of permanently settled Bengal, and of the hitherto periodically leased North-West, is thus described by a native traveller from the former Province:—

"As we proceeded, everything about us bespoke of Hindoostan—the stalwart and muscular men, their turbaned heads and tucked-up *dhooties*, their Hindu colloquy, the *garment wearing women*, the mud-roofed houses, the fields of *jowara*, the dry soil and air, the superior cattle, the camels, the absence of the bamboo and cocoa, and the wells in places of tanks. In sea-board Bengal, bogs, fens and forests cover nearly a third of its area. In the Doab, almost every inch of land is under the plough. From Allahabad to Shekoabad, there are four large cities and villages at frequent intervals. A similar distance in Bengal is no doubt dotted with the same number of villages, but not one town equal to Futtehpore, Cawnpore, or Mynpooree. There townships deserving of the name occur only along the banks of the Bhagirutty. If villages in the Doab are less picturesque, they are at the same time less subject to epidemics than the woody villages of Bengal. In a Bengal village, hardly any better food is generally procurable than coarse rice, and lentils, and *goor*. In the rural districts of the Doab, flour, vegetables, fruits, milk and sweet-meats are as abundant and excellent as in a metropolis. The food of a people is the best criterion of its condition. Here, the rural population is more intelligent and spirited than the same class in Bengal. The ryot in Hindoostan is no less a bondsman to the *mahajun* than the ryot in Jessore or Dacca. But he is more independent-minded, and would not tamely put up with the outrages that are inflicted by a Bengal Zemindar, or indigo planter. Unquestionably, the humblest Doabee lives upon better food, and covers his body with more abundant clothing than the humblest Bengalee. The cattle here are various. Camels, buffaloes, horses, donkeys and oxen are all made to assist man in his labours. In Bengal, the oxen alone form beasts of burden. The fashion of Hindoostanee cooleyism is to take the load over the waist, and not upon the head. In Calcutta, the Baboos who talk big of politics and reformations, do not know what it is to ride. In Hindoostan, rural women perform journeys on horseback, and princesses discuss the merits of horsemanship. The fondness of the Doabee women for coloured millinery, certainly evinces a more refined female taste, and to them may remotely be traced the impetus which is given to the various dye manufactures of our country. The agricultural women of Doab use ornaments of brass and bell-metal. The same class in Bengal is in the habit of wearing shell-ornaments—ornaments that first came into fashion with the savages, though sometimes a pair of Dacca shell bracelets may cost the sum of 250 rupees."*

And, if this was the case when the Baboo wrote, which from internal evidence seems to have been about five years ago, what must be the contrast between the two provinces, now that at last *Famine*, in its most appalling form, has fallen upon Bengal! An unprecedentedly protracted drought has been followed by excessive deluges of unseasonable rain, and prices are about ten times their normal rate. How Bengal was prepared to meet it, let the following extract from the writings of one of the most able and consistent advocates of the permanent settlement express: it contained "millions of

* "Trips and Tours," published in the *Saturday Evening Englishman*, Calcutta, 1866. The present writer is responsible for nothing but the *italics*.

ignorant squatters, whom we will not educate, and who so live from hand to mouth, that when rain fails, famine sweeps them away." Such is the present candid admission of the *Friend of India*.* When the famine came, there were no preparations, and people were "swept away" like rubbish. In the North-West and the Punjab, where the Government, being the universal landlord of the whole country, has always felt the necessity of providing the great improvements which they alone had the will or the power to carry out, and had always taken a direct interest in the people, how different was the result. Roads speedily conveyed grain from places where it was abundant to the scenes of dearth, and the high prices not only drew forth all necessary supplies from the tracts watered by canals for those who could not travel, but enabled the holders of such lands to provide employment for numbers of able-bodied labourers from famine-stricken districts, who came to them for temporary service.

* Orissa itself is not permanently settled; but the famine was at first no worse there than in other parts of Bengal, which are. The subsequent prominence given to Orissa, is caused by the continuance of bad crops there after the seasons in Bengal had returned to their due courses.

Such were some of the salient points of contrast between the state of the masses under a permanent settlement, and under one in which the State remained landlord, with a power of raising its leases periodically.*

But, as the former system has now been promised as a "boon" to the people at large, it will be well to notice that, for evil or for good, the time-honoured finance of the East is dead for India, and we must now bestir ourselves seriously to provide some means of direct taxation, or look for other relief to the threatened finances. Taxes proper, unlike the land revenue of India, all fall eventually upon the consumers, the majority of whom must always be poor, and every system of taxation may be regarded as a more or less successful buffer, introduced to break the blow. Probably the least oppressive form of tax for this country, where, except the ill-starred income-tax of 1860, direct taxation for State purposes is almost unknown, would be some sort of *graduated capitation*, like what was introduced into France in the last century, and

* Note especially the account given by the Bengalee writer quoted above of his surprise at finding the *women clothed*, the *land* all *cultivated*, and *numerous large cities* about the country.

which was only prevented from being the restoration of French finance, by the fatal obstinacy with which the privileged classes resisted its extension to themselves. By exempting the poorest class, and making the richer pay in some kind of ratio to their means, an average of one rupee per adult male might be obtainable annually, which would yield about £4,000,000 sterling to the yearly revenue, or three-fold the amount of the late income-tax, and increase the general rate of taxation about three annas (say four pence halfpenny) per head.* Another measure of relief might be obtained by relegating to the Local Governments certain items of expenditure heretofore borne by the general resources of the Supreme Government, but which, to the amount of nearly four and three-quarter millions, belong to matters of administration in which the localities are chiefly versed and interested, such are "Allowances to village and district officers," "Administration and Public Departments," "Education," and

* On the unpopularity of the income-tax among the Natives, see Note at the end of this chapter. But, perhaps the worst feature of this, now happily departed impost, was, that its main incidence fell upon the Europeans, official and non-official, whose real incomes could be alone ascertained.

"Police;" any or all of which could form part of the local budgets, and be provided for by the Local Governments, under such restrictions as might appear proper as to the methods of raising them. When I said above, that direct taxation to the State was almost unknown, I intended to exclude municipal levies, with which the people are perfectly familiar, and which, being spent in their presence and for their benefit, are not so odious as imperial imposts. The people have a rooted idea, that the British Government is always sending their money to Europe; and the less we tax them for purposes they do not understand, the less unpopular we are likely to be.*

I have said much about Revenue, yet I can hardly hope to have done much towards recommending my views to those who are of an opposite way of thinking. The questions of pure finance yet remain; but on the eve of action being taken upon the Report of the Commission appointed by Sir John Lawrence, I hesitate to express an opinion. One thing, indeed, is patent to every one in the country, Sir C. Wood's Paper Currency, like most of

* *Vide* Note at the end of this Chapter, already referred to.

the measures exported to us from England, was a *misfit;* there has been hardly any increase of the circulation of notes, over what obtained under the old system; indeed, the failure of the scheme is admitted in the appointment of the Commission of Inquiry. How far a system of small Exchequer bills,* bearing interest, and only convertible at the Treasury from which they were issued, might answer, this is hardly the place to inquire—only this much may be craved, that we be allowed in future to do our own financing, under due responsibility. It is often said that finance was one of the weakest points of the local administration. Nothing can be more false. Deficits were constant; but so were wars, and the secret of making war support itself appears to be far from widely divulged. In times of peace we usually had a nett surplus, *besides sending home a tribute,* which has never, in modern times, been less than three millions, and which, as shown above, is now about eight, of which between five and six millions give to India no return whatever.

* *Vide* Appendix II.

NOTE.—The Bengalee writer, from whom we have above borrowed an account of the different aspects of Bengal and the north-west, also furnishes an interesting picture of the Hindoostanee feeling, when the Income Tax was being levied. He is describing a visit that he paid to an "up-country" friend at Agra:—

"Nothing could have been more welcome after the long day's touring and sight-seeing, than to sit to the excellent supper got up by our host—a pleasant sequel to sum up one of the most pleasant days of our life. The supper was in a style to tempt a Catholic to break through his Lent. The conversation turned upon the principal subject of the day—Income-Tax. Throughout Hindoostan it is regarded as a national mulct for the rebellion. The mysterious 'wants of the State' are incomprehensible to the popular understanding. As yet, the Indians have not a common national mind to feel a concern or the welfare of a common State. They are busy about their own private fiscal prosperity, and indifferent to any outside calls of common interest. It never enters into their thoughts to inquire about the annual income or expenditure of the State—or to care about its 'chronic deficits.' The eloquent English of our Financier has told upon a limited number, but has scarcely enlightened the mass of the population, beyond making this much distinction, that their pockets are to be touched, not by any force of arms, but by the force of arguments. Familiar only with the Land-Tax and customs, our nation needs the political education to be prepared for the innovation of a higher political science. Never before was the National Debt known in India, where only the whim of a despot had to be pledged for its payment. Not more is the National Debt foreign to the ideas of the north-westerns than is the Income-Tax. The native mind must be taught to appreciate the wants of the State—to feel an interest in its well-being, before it will endorse the opinion that 'Taxation is no tyranny.' "—"*Trips and Tours*," *Englishman's Weekly Journal*. Calcutta, 1866.

LETTER VI.

OF THE SAME (JUSTICE.)

Not far inferior in importance to Finance in the eyes of an eastern people is the administration of justice. All readers of jest-books will remember how many of the oriental anecdotes turn upon the acuteness of the "Cadi," or the impartiality of Nowsheerwan, the just King of Persia. In fact, in a country where moral and social obligations are chiefly confined to the tribe or family, it would be impossible for the inhabitants to be kept at all decently within the limits of peace and propriety and social duty, without a strong judicial system. In the anarchy which preceded our occupation of Hindoostan, every country, every hundred, almost every village, contained within itself the elements of civil war. Now that a strong hand has composed these, the traditional instincts of combat find a bloodless arena in the law courts. Unfounded claims and complaints are met by baseless *alibis* and counter-charges; chosen companions from one tribe, offering themselves freely to the chances of punishment for perjury, oppose their false evidence to the false evidence of the representatives of the hostile tribe; if the witnesses on one side swear that black is white, those on the other are equally ready to swear that, on the contrary, white is black.

In such a state of society,—and let those who know it best say whether the picture is overcoloured,—a sound judicial system is of the last importance.

The following description of the Bengal system is believed to be, in the main, applicable to those of the other presidencies.

Throughout the Bengal presidency there are two systems existing side by side: the one subject in all things to the judicial supervision of High Courts of Judicature, (which have succeeded to the old Sudder Courts), the other in which there is no distinction, in point of *personnel*, in any grade, between judiciary and executive.

Under the Regulation system, which is general through Madras, Bombay, Bengal, and the North-West, with the exception of certain acquisitions of territory of a comparatively modern date, the supreme tribunal is, as above said, the High Court, composed (with a single exception) of European Judges, who have risen either at the English and Presidency Bars, or in the routine of the Civil Service. The duties of these courts are to administer justice in certain cases, and to supervise the administration of it in others by the Provincial Courts. The courts immediately below them again are presided over by officers whose duties are of the same character, and purely judicial. But unlike the High Court Judges, who are, to a certain extent, trained lawyers, the second grade, or District Judges, are all men who have learned their work in the discharge of duties chiefly administrative. Below these occurs a bifurcation; Civil Justice, for the most part, is originally administered by Native Judges, men whose youth has been passed in the calling of a Pleader, or as ministerial officers of the courts; but cases between landlord and tenant regarding land are heard before the officers whose primary duty it is to look after the collection of the land revenue, and the same persons are generally also entrusted with powers corresponding at once to those of Justices of the Peace, and to those of courts of Quarter Sessions. The limit of a magistrate's jurisdiction is two years, with hard labour, and a fine; but within that limit he acts alone, without either bench or jury. In many instances he is also Chief of the Police.

To these must be added, in regard to Civil Justice, a few courts, resembling the County Courts of England, vested with limited powers for the determination of causes arising out of small debts; and certain subordinate tribunals under Native officials for the trial of cases of Revenue and correctional matters; a few rich landholders have also been made Honorary Magistrates.

In the Punjab, a mixed system prevails. There is a Chief Court, of which one of the members is an English lawyer, but the judges of the courts below are all officers, many of them taken from the Army, who are in the active discharge of executive functions. In Oudh, Scinde, the Central Provinces, Mysore, Hydrabad, Assam, and the Sonthal country, the mixture of the executive and judicial functions is still more complete.

The whole of these systems, Regulation and Non-regulation, are in different degrees open to the same criticism. In some more, in others less, a vast number of the judiciary body need not have had a professional training, need not have the whole of their time and powers devoted to administering justice, and are liable to have their attention distracted, and perhaps their fairness warped, by the multifarious duties of a Chief Constable, a Land Bailiff, a Road Trustee, and a Municipal Commissioner. Finally, with the exception of the High Courts, each officer sits *alone* and (saving only the Small Cause Courts, where everything is sacrificed to speed) the errors inseparable from crotchet, caprice, or incompetence are checked by a ramification of appeals, which is fatal to certainty, and pregnant with delay. One of the most recent and widely-noticed schemes for the reformation of Indian justice is that put forth by Sir Erskine Perry, whose proposed Bill is, in a few words, to make use of existing elements, and to carry the amalgamation pattern of the High Courts down to a lower level. He would appoint the fittest man, Native or European, covenanted or uncovenanted, and he would unite all the existing courts in a district into one court, over which a "Chief Judge," usually a Barrister, should preside (and which would, I presume, be divided into benches for the simultaneous discharge of different kinds of duty.)

Now I think this plan, in its present form, neither very feasible nor very efficient. The Barrister Chief will bring to the Bench a vast amount of that "greenness," which, rendering authority ridiculous, is a blunder worse than a crime. He may, or he may not, also bring a knowledge of English law, which is generally admitted by thinking men to be one of the worst in the world, and of the practice and procedure of Westminster Hall, which is borne with impatience in its own country, and not at all needed here. And, lastly, he will be often a briefless and brainless failure, who owes his appointment to purely personal and corrupt considerations.

In the rare cases in which the chief is a native of India, he will want moral and social weight; and confusion will surge below him, till he drifts like Carlyle's "dead donkey on a deluge of mud." And when he happens to be a covenanted civilian, the circumstance will be constantly thrown in his teeth.

But besides this, the existing system has certain claims to our confidence. In the first place, it has *grown up*; it is not a spick-and-span system just invented by some clever closetteer, and started as an experiment *in corpore vili*. In the next place, it is an advantage that many of the higher officers belong to a service with high traditions and great social and pecuniary advantages, which give a considerable guarantee for their honour and impartiality; and, lastly, they have passed through an apprenticeship of practical acquaintance with the wants and ways of the people, which makes them, to a considerable extent, independent of experts and interpreters. It is more important to an Indian judge to know a native language than to know English law.

Other objections have been brought forward in India against details of this Bill, amongst which the most deserving of notice, perhaps, is that candidly admitted by the *Indian Jurist*, a well-conducted organ of the lawyers of Calcutta, which is honest in allowing that the plan involves a sweeping blow at the vested rights of those members of the Civil Service who have won their posts by competitive examination. These gentlemen have entered the service on the understanding that judicial prizes were open to them; sufficient time has not yet elapsed to give them an opportunity of proving thier fitness for the duties of an Indian Judge; and in the meantime it would be contrary to all English precedent to introduce a revolution that would confiscate their just expectations.

Much of this reasoning must, I think, be admitted to be just; but there is still that in Sir Erskine's plan which merits attentive consideration. The necessary correction required at once to meet those objections which are tenable, and to give the reform a fair scope seems to be the erection of a *separate department* of the Civil Service for judicial work, as has been already done by Lord Canning in the department of finance. This is a local reform, and, like the best portions of Sir Erskine Perry's scheme, can be carried out without the necessity of any reference to the imperial parliament. I do not think the introduction of the barrister element would work well. I do not think that it is shown to be called for, and this being the case, I do not think it would be fair. The many and glaring deficiencies of the old Civil Service in this department certainly call for *some* guarantee for the future; but, looking to the circumstances of this country, I am sure we could never reckon upon a sufficient supply of well-qualified barristers. On the other hand, I am equally convinced that a well-educated young man, who has been conscientiously engaged for five years as assistant to a district officer, will bring to the trial of nearly every kind of case that could come before him on the Mofussil bench, a number of most important qualifications. Only provision ought, in my humble opinion, to be made, as in finance is now done, that no officers enter the special department that have not shown special marks of fitness; when once selected for the Bench, they should neither be teased nor tempted with any incompatible duties; and lastly, none but trifling cases, either on the civil or the criminal side, should be disposed of by a single judge. Whatever appeals were still considered necessary should be disposed of by at least two judges, of whom it would be well that the original trying officer should be one.

The officers thus excluded from the bench would not be injured, nor would any slight be thrown upon them. Many a man, who is more suited for the woolsack than the pig-skin, would be at a *nonplus* in the hundred matters that daily demand the promptest decision of the administration of an Indian district. Some of our best district officers on the other hand are well known to look forward with anguish to the day when, in the course of seniority, they must be made judges. In Madras, this is partially obviated by the equalization of pay, a district officer drawing the same as a judge; and there can be little doubt that the public service would be largely benefitted if the principle could be extended to all parts of India and to every grade of administration. Nor need the employment of natives, that most important step in the popularization of our rule, be in any degree hindered by what is here proposed. The lower courts of first instance might still continue to be presided over by men of all classes, care being taken that no uncovenanted man was appointed who had not received a real forensic training. Practically the scheme would work thus. Every covenanted writer, on passing the college of Fort William, would pass an apprenticeship of five years in the general or administrative line. At the expiry of that period, he would be called on to pass an examination in one or two departments; either the financial, the administrative (including police and non-judicial revenue work) or in the duties of the bench, the law of evidence, and the procedure codes. A certificate from his superior officer, stating the line for which the candidate was best qualified, should also be submitted, and in the extreme case of an officer possessing a certificate for one line insisting on going in for the other, the final decision should rest with the local Government. The barrier of judicial examination once crossed, our aspirant might, in the first instance, be posted, as registrar or clerk of the court to a district judge, under whom he would obtain his first practical acquaintance with the working of the system. As vacancies occurred, he would have a chance of competing for judicial promotion with the celebrities of the local bar; just as is now the case in regard to the judgeships of small cause courts; but the controlling and appellate jurisdiction of a district court should, as a matter of fairness and expediency, be reserved, as at present, for the covenanted alone. Brilliant merit in the uncovenanted ranks might perhaps be occasionally rewarded by the gift of a covenant appointment, but this would require to be carefully watched, and, like the bestowal of commissions in the army on deserving serjeants, should be referred in each case for the sanction of the crown.

NOTE. I am proud to be able to cite in support of the views advanced in this letter the advice tendered to Sir H. B. Frere, on his retirement from the government of Bombay, by the chief justice of the high court there, himself a distinguished barrister-judge:—

"No class of young men can be imported from England better fitted for the successful administration of justice in the Mofussil than the class of civilians who are now coming out to us—young men well grounded in the general principles of jurisprudence, completely versed in the vernaculars, ready, as far as the exigencies of the service will permit, to devote themselves exclusively to a judicial career. I want His Excellency to carry that opinion home with him, to be slung, as occasion may serve, in the Indian Council, against that redoubtable Goliath of the trained barrister interest, my honourable and learned predecessor, Sir Erskine Perry." (Laughter and applause.)—*Speech of Sir J. Arnould, at farewell dinner to Governor Frere, Bombay, 14th February,* 1867.

LETTER VII.

OF THE SAME. POLICE, EDUCATION, THE CIVIL SERVICE, SALARIES.

CLOSELY coupled with justice, and not less important to the public welfare, is the administration of the police. The old system, in most parts of British India, was briefly this: the constabulary was under the control of native officers who got very small pay, and who were again supervised by the European representative of Government, whom we have already met in these pages as the district officer, but whose official title in Madras, the North-west, and Bombay, was "magistrate and collector," the revenue functions being for the most part separate in Bengal Proper. Into the various evils of this system it is not now necessary to enter in detail; suffice it to say, that the corruption of the lower grades, the perfunctionary supervision of the higher, and the unseemly confusion of judicial and executive duties in the hands of the magistrate and his assistants, led to the gradual introduction, first into Madras, and subsequently into all India, of the modified Irish system first naturalized in Sindh, when that province was administered by the late Sir C. J. Napier. But the police reform has not hitherto met the very first of the objections to the old system, in consequence of the department having been allowed to revert gradually to the control of judicial officers. I have above expressed my sense of the weakness introduced into our judicial system by the blending of functions in the case at least of the higher European officials, which was perhaps unavoidable in the rough-and-ready administration of newly-acquired territory. But this, as society grows, is felt a particular, not to say insurmountable, obstacle to efficiency in the department that we are now considering. It seems at first sight bad enough that an officer should be called upon to decide upon the disputes of landlord and tenant, or to dispose of nice technicalities in the penal code, at a time when his prospects in the service depend upon his making good roads, and keeping down the inefficient balance in his treasury. But it is still worse, and a scandal to our system, that he may also be in charge of the police of his district or his subdivision, appears, as it were, as a party in his own court, and condemn the prisoner whom his own detective energies have, rightly or wrongly, placed at the bar. To any one who cannot see the force of this argument, I would put a practical question, and ask, why it is that our judicial system has to be undermined with a honeycomb of appeals, unless by reason of the want of confidence in the lower courts, of which the knowledge of the above facts is the cause? If the police really and truly prosecuted every person arraigned before an Indian magistrate, and every sentence above six months had to be signed by three officers, there would be no more need for appeals on the facts of cases than there is in England, and the voluminous record and the uncertain administration would vanish out of sight together. This preliminary requisition will be met by the proposed erection of a separate judicial department. But it is evident that more is wanted before the police can be rendered thoroughly efficient. It is clearly not *money*, however, that is first needed. No false economy actuated the introducers of the new system. The amount devoted to this service, which but slightly varied between 1835 and 1850, has, in the second fifteen years, risen 50 per cent. upon the former amount. The estimate for 1866-7 shows a still further increase.

1835-36.	1849-50.	1864-65.
1,631,000	1,943,550	2,361,011

Yet complaints continue to be made. The natives are the most affected by this, and the opinions of the natives are not easily made known. But there is no denying that they are dissatisfied. Criminals may not be tortured, but crime is not kept down. The same is understood to be the complaint in Ireland, the police being too exclusively military, the detective element languishes. In India this is certainly the case—Mr. Waterfield's report for last year shows the same note in almost all the provinces—"Crime on the increase." Whether the separation of the judicial duties entirely from the control of the police* would improve the one as much as the other, it would perhaps

* While I write this, a measure is being introduced, experimentally, into a part of the lower provinces; but the mischief is, that the district officer will revert, on promotion, to the judicial line. The two departments should be wholly distinct.

be rash to predict. Much must always depend upon the principle which guides the selection of the controlling officers; but I believe that the best officer will work badly if he is constantly exposed to interference on the part of another officer, who is not his departmental superior and has not his departmental knowledge.

The only remaining feature of local administration with which I have here any necessity to deal is that of education. Here, again, a most injudicious increase of expenditure is taking place. This department, which had no separate existence in the balance sheet previous to Lord Canning's reign, received upwards of half a million sterling in 1864-65, and the estimate for the coming year goes over three-quarters of a million.* That more should be spent is, perhaps, unadvisable in the present unprosperous state of the instructional system thus provided for.

The main proof, that the present system does

* To this must be added local cesses, private donations, subscriptions, fees, and grants from municipal funds, of which no record is given by Mr. Waterfield, but which cannot aggregate less than a corresponding sum, or a million and a half in all this service.

not succeed, is that, in spite of the constant instructions of the various local Governments, the higher officials cannot, or will not, fill vacancies in their offices by pupils from State schools. Various opinions have been expressed as to the propriety of bribing the people to send their sons to school with the promise of public employment before their education is finished; but it cannot be doubted that all impartial and intelligent heads of departments and offices would, for the sake of their own reputations, seek eagerly for the alumni of governmental institutions, if they found them much superior to other natives. That they do not do this is clear from the complaints of the various inspectors and the remonstrances and injunctions of the local Governments.

Another disappointing thing is, that though the system of State education has been at work on a considerable scale for the past ten years, not only does Christianity make no progress, but the fanaticism and superstition of the people in the country at large, and with due exceptions as regards great centres of civilisation like Calcutta and Bombay, appear not at all abated. Crime, as above said, is on the increase, and the best native judges and pleaders, as far as the experience of the writer goes, are still men who have been trained in the learning of their fathers, and not at all, or but slightly, in our schools and colleges. The flaw was pointed out many years ago by a writer, now a Pusine Judge of the Calcutta High Court, and who has seen the educated native in almost every part of India, in words which time has unfortunately not deprived of their force:—"A great many young Hindoos have been taught Milton, and made proficient in a literature which they will never appreciate; but few have learned the *practical science* for which their genius so eminently fits them."—(*Campbell's Modern India*, p. 190.)

To a people possessed of a highly imaginative poetry, and a highly transcendental metaphysic, but ignorant as animals of the laws of Nature, and supremely indifferent to fact, we give Shakespeare and Bacon, and Kant and Hegel, together with a *quant. suff.* of pure mathematics: can we wonder at the result? or complain if the highly accomplished men that we tempt from the English universities to cary out this system, manifest that utter dissatisfaction with it which is well known to all who have the privilege of their acquaintance, or take the trouble to read the various periodicals which they conduct?

One of these organs* lately put forth the following protest against the fundamental notions of educ tion which pervade our present system:—

"We trust that we have shown that it would not be desirable to Europeanize the peoples of this country. For some 'practical' readers it may be as well to add the suggestion, that it would also be impossible. There is no instance that we can call to mind of a nation in any degree advanced beyond the condition of savages being induced to adopt the thoughts and habits of foreign conquerors. What neither the hard legalism of the ancient Romans was able to do for the people of Britain or Asia Minor, nor the powerful machinery of the Spanish Church to carry out among the peoples of Mexico and Peru, is hardly likely to be achieved by the half-hearted and self-questioning convictions of modern England. To borrow an illustration from material science, the propagation of opinion must be endemic, not epidemic."

Of course, it may be argued, that the civilisation of the countries mentioned was not wholly

* *Agra and Delhi Educational Magazine*, 1866.

unaffected by their conquerors. But it is impossible to say that the natives of America were affected *beneficially* by what they learned from the Spaniards, the *virtues* of the Spanish character have not been imparted to them; and the last state of those men is worse than the first. Better would it be for India that she had never come under British influence than that she should ever be inhabited by races like the present descendants of the subjects of Montezuma and the Incas. Yet that some such result would follow the success of the educational system inaugurated by British philanthropy in India, no true student of history can doubt. The institutions of a country are the results of its climate, and other physical characteristics; and the British oak is but a feeble exotic when transplanted to the banks of the Ganges.

We have seen that the officers of the educational service are dissatisfied. I fear that this is not the case with them alone, but extends to all the men of culture and high aims whom the recent changes have brought to India. Drs. Johnson and Southey both spoke strongly in old times of the social and intellectual privations to which such men would be subject in India; but in their days such were not the qualities of first necessity for the Indian officials. Indeed, down to quite late times, not only were the Civil Officers sent out men of, generally speaking, inferior culture, but they were in numerous instances men who had been born in the country and only sent home for their education. All were more or less connected with the country, and became, on their arrival, members of a sort of "happy family," which looked upon the country as its own. Very different is the case of the modern "Competition-Wallah." Educated at an English school or college, never thinking, it may be, of India, till he is seventeen or eighteen; knowing few of his contemporaries, and still fewer of his seniors, he moves in India as an exile in a strange land. Some, deficient, perhaps, in early physical training, die of disappointment and the climate, others retire, while those who remain, if not speedily selected for appointments of an exceptionally agreeable character, linger on in a half-hearted pining condition, and perhaps do their best to deter their relations and friends at home from following their footsteps. *See* the subjoined extract from the leading journal of this part of India, the Calcutta *Englishman* of September 24, 1866:—

"We recently recorded the resignation of three young civilians, including one of the most successful Small Cause Court Judges that we have had, and there are many others willing to follow their example.

"The effects which we long ago predicted are now taking place, and the English public have realised the fact, that the Indian Civil Service is no career for a University man. A few years since we noticed that graduates were ceasing to come out; but now no one who is able to pay for a University education, whether he be a graduate or an under-graduate, is willing to compete. So far as we remember, there is not a single young gentleman in the list of candidates last selected who has had the advantages of a University training, and several of the best men who have come out are only waiting till their furlough gives them a year at home, in which to look about for a new employment."

To these, perhaps, unavoidable disadvantages must be added that, owing to the constant fall in the value of money already described, the salaries are not now what they were, while the value of the service is further deteriorated by occasional threats of throwing open the more lucrative posts. It is not only possible, but has actually happened, that a young lawyer from England can be put *at once* upon a salary of £5,000 a year in a position which the civilian cannot dream of until he has been twenty years in the country. Yet when a local Government lately applied for an increase of salaries, the application was sternly negatived; while it was all that the Governor-General could do last year to prevent a still further reduction. It is poor economy to put your dogs and horses on half rations, and one that could only be contemplated by an absentee landlord.

Again, the leave rules are fantastically barbarous. A man in the Civil Service can only get a furlough of three years in his whole career, and that by vacating his appointment; while he has to pay his passage both ways, and keep himself and family in England on £500 a year! As for leave in India, he can have that likewise once during his service, and then only for six months, which do not count towards retirement. Finally, after twenty-five years' service, he is at liberty to retire upon an annuity of £1,000 a year, for which he has to pay £5,000, and of which the remaining value is largely supplied by the forfeited payments of deceased fellow-servants. It can hardly be doubted that, as in the case of the military officers, these grievances must be redressed some day, but the local Government would do it sooner and to more purpose than a House of Commons of squires and railway directors, who neither know nor care about Indian civil officers.

LETTER VIII.

OF THE VICEROY'S POWERS.

Having thus briefly sketched the position and possibilities of Indian administration as regards home and foreign relations (so called,) it remains to apply a similar process to the ostensible head of this complicated system. What is the Viceroy, and of what beneficial action does his office admit? Is he merely a decorative part of the system required to represent the incarnate Majesty of Britain in Durbars and Councils, but with no more real power of governing than if he were an intelligent telegraph signaller stationed at Calcutta to register orders from the Secretary of State's Office? A late No. of the *Quarterly Review*, in an article reminding one very much of the crude, though clever, speeches of men who "go in for India" in the House of Commons, takes the last-named view without hesitation; and Tory though he be, the author boldy attributes all the recent progress of India to "the careful and enlightened administration of Sir Charles Wood."—(*Quarterly Review*, *No.* 239, *July*, 1866.)

Now this view, however attractive from its simplicity, is clearly open to some almost annihilating contradictions from fact. In the first place a great many of Lord Halifax's measures have broken down: notably, the Army amalgamation, with all its attendant details, which has only lately, after about eight years' tinkering, been put to rights by the Conservative Cabinet: also the Paper Currency, the Income-Tax, and the attempt to reduce civil salaries. Secondly, some of the greatest improvements in the Indian Commonwealth are due to the impetus of Lord Dalhousie, or to the long and careful preparations of the Court of Directors,—I allude especially to the spread of education, and the extension of railroads and telegraphs. Other reforms, that have chronologically followed the Mutiny, had been either got ready long before by Indian officials, like the Penal and Procedure Codes, or had been provided for, like other measures of Law Reform, by the local

Council in Calcutta. In short, an important and beneficial measure, which owes its existence to the late Secretary, would be quite an exceptional phenomenon. Lower down the Reviewer distinctly expresses himself in the strongest possible terms on this subject:—"The Government is entirely the Government of England. . . . . In England the taxation is determined . . . . and by England the duties on the trade between the two countries are determined.* In short, though the whole cost of the Government is imposed upon India, India is governed by the English Ministry through Her Majesty's Secretary of State."

In another place he gives a description of the late Legislative Council, and another of the Council in its present modified form; but in his eagerness to prove that they are a mere set of official dummies, he quite omits to mention the existence of non-official members, either Native or European. Finally, he says:—"If it were more clearly understood that the real Government of India is the people of England through the Queen's Ministry and Parliament; that there is no other Government; that the

* This should be, but is not always the case.

Governor-General and his Council are but their" (the people's) "nominees; and that the solvency of the Indian Exchequer is the solvency of the Crown of England—there could not be," &c.* Yet it cannot be denied that the Reviewer has correctly stated the theory, with a few errors of detail, on which the Government of India is supposed to be carried on; and also, that not only in theory, but even in point of fact, the administrative control of the English Cabinet over Indian affairs is far stronger, and more direct, than what it exercises over any colony, pure and simple. The distinction which the Reviewer draws between a colony and a conquered country, is in the main just, but in its *statement* there is just this omission, that a Province of this sort is apt to acquire gradually colonial tendencies, while in its *application*, it must be borne in mind that even a parish has an autonomy as to the state of the church clock; and even so a conquered Province, however dependent, must needs have some power over its domestic affairs. The wearer of a shoe will do something to mitigate its pinch, under pain of being condemned to go for ever barefoot.

* Would that it were so; that we could borrow money at less than five per cent.

But the evils of the present system may all be summed up by saying that it is faulty just where the old "double government" was faulty. The experienced persons in India, who do the greater part of the work, are never seen, scarcely *heard* of: fame and fortune rarely crown them when successful, and the blame of their failure is sure to rest on others. I am far from thinking that the local administration has not power enough. I think, considering the *kind* of work that it does, and its freedom from responsibility, that it has *in practice* too much. Who in England ever heard of John Colvin or Henry Torrens? and yet those unknown Under-Secretaries determined the undertaking of Lord Auckland's Cabul expedition, which cost us so much blood and treasure, and has formed a standing topic of reproach against the Home Government ever since. The Home Government, forsooth! There has hardly been one war in India, for good or for evil, that Indian Governors, instigated often by obscure officials, did not set agoing with such vigour, that the Court of Directors and Board of Control, compromised and almost paralysed, could do nothing but imitate the hen, who shrieks from the shore when her foster brood of ducklings have plunged into the water. I ask pardon for the homely simile; but if this does not express a constant attitude of the Government and people of England on such occasions, then their endorsement of conduct, like Lord Wellesley's attack upon the Tranco-Mahratta power in 1802, or Lord Ellenborough's attack on Sindh in later days, must be set down to worse motives. Lord Ellenborough was recalled, it is true, as Lord Wellesley had been very near being; but none of their acts were disavowed, nor any of their spoils restored to the former owners. Now, at all events, since the abolition of the Company's power, India is not, and cannot, be really governed in England. The notorious apathy of Parliament renders that impossible, nor has any promising method of removing that apathy ever been pointed out. The Secretary of State has a most experienced and efficient Council; but its vigour is sapped by the law that excludes its members from the council of the nation; and there are no senators left who have the requisite knowledge and weight.

Take as an instance the recent history of the Mysore question, as described in the following extract from a journal always well informed on Indian matters. Here we see the complete divorce between knowledge and power. The Parliament which has the power, not wishing to understand the question, the Council that has the knowledge, not able to act :—

"Sir Charles Wood was by no means a popular minister, and yet, without one protest from Parliament, and barely one protest from the English press, he was allowed to commit himself to a measure of annexation, which, in the opinion of those who know India best and have her interests at heart, will affect the welfare and even the security of our whole Indian empire, by spreading terror and distrust among the Native States. Until a deputation on the subject went up the other day to Lord Cranborne, no public protest had been made. This silence, moreover, was maintained by Parliament in face of the fact that, even by his own Council, here in England, Sir Charles Wood was vigorously opposed."—(*Daily News, August 2nd*, 1866.)

With Parliament thus indifferent, and the special Council so weak, it is not easy to see how the Indian Minister can be properly checked, stimulated, or supported, so as to govern India effectually.

On the other hand, take the Viceroy, not as

described by the *Quarterly*, a timid, aristocratic placeman, surrounded by nominee advisers, but (as we see from the present case he may be) a ripe, public man, versed in his youth in every detail of Indian administration, yet imbued, during some fruitful years of later manhood, with the enlightened principles of English statesmanship; standing conspicuously forth, in the sight of all men, with his head still waiting its final decoration from his country; surrounded by advisers, equally responsible with himself, and selected not alone from amongst experienced officials, but also from grave merchants, and Native Chiefs of distinguished merit; and lastly, bearing in his hands the scales, in which the reputation of every subordinate administrator is weighed, and the power of rewarding or punishing each one accordingly; and say if this is not the man who will be the real ruler of the country? Why, the very *patronage* alone makes him omnipotent. Who amongst his subordinate agents, the Commissioners and District Officers, who really act upon the people, will dare to transgress the lines of a man's policy, who can, with one stroke of the pen, raise them to quasi-royalty or humble them to an office-stool? What cares a revenue officer for the supposed bias of a member of some ministry at home, who may lose office to-morrow, in opposition to a half-sheet of foolscap from the Simla Secretariat?

The consequences of this are curious. Parliament and the constituencies at home, pressed by complicated local cares, and not quite sure who is responsible about India, or who is right,—getting a budget statement from Calcutta in May, and another from Victoria Street in August,—exact, in ordinary times, but little justification from any person connected with India. On the other hand, in this country, two classes exercise an important and interested vigilance over the local rulers. The European community, official, commercial, and to a limited extent agricultural, watch the Governor-General with eagerness, and criticise him *à la loupe*, as may be seen from the discontents, of which the majority of Anglo-Indian journals are the medium. The Natives, long accustomed to have despotism brought home to their own doors, and by nature given to the concrete, weigh the character and conduct of the officers who *immediately* sway their destinies, but they likewise regard the Viceroy with awe, in which confidence is mixed, while they do not realize the Home Government in any form the least capable of expression, and the Viceroy, for his part, never gives his assent to a Bill of any importance, until he has first done his best to elicit Native opinion.

Lord Cranborne's inaugural speech showed that his acuteness and fine sense have shown him something of this; and should his thought become as fruitful as is likely, we may hope to see a remedy introduced into the present chaotic condition of the body politic. To enforce peace, to encourage public works, and to protect the Native princes, these are the very points which are clearly within the province of an Imperial centre, but have been most indifferently managed by all previous Ministers. Tied down to these general principles, and prohibited from interfering with export or import dues, which might affect the commerce of the empire, a Viceroy might then be made as completely independent in theory (as to what we may call parochial affairs) as he must always be in practice, and at the same time be rendered as responsible to England as he is already conspicuous in India.

NOTE.—When Lord Canning issued his famous Proclamation, confiscating all the land in Oudh, numbers of influential men in both Houses were ready to stand forward in his defence, against the censures of the Cabinet. Who would Sir John Lawrence have to support him, supposing Lord Cranborne should disapprove of the way in which that question has been finally settled? So that we are in this position, that a Viceroy who has risen from the ranks of civil administration, where he has acquired experience and proved desert, cannot do what a nobleman fresh from home can do with almost certain immunity. In other words, a Viceroy's independence is in inverse ratio to his fitness.

LETTER IX.

OF THE IMPERIAL SYSTEM. AS IT IS, AND AS IT MIGHT BE.

As my task draws to its close, I am anxious once more to explain its nature. I am not so vain as to think that in these few pages I can have given such a panorama of Indian affairs as to carry conviction upon any point of detail. I shall be abundantly satisfied if those who may have lent me their indulgence so far, have been interested in my general view of the problem. We have begun to perceive that, while the local administrators of British India have often done mischief, by being left to initiate measures for which they have not been held duly responsible, on the other hand, the interference of the Home Government has been sometimes inoperative and sometimes mischievous. I have not concealed my conviction, that this danger has much increased since all power has been taken from the experts. When the retired Indians had some chance of stamping their own policy on the affairs of India, and were able to stand up in Parliament and defend that policy before the British nation, the system, like many other English systems, was deficient in certainty and symmetry; but, at any rate, Parliament had no excuse for not knowing what was going on. If, contrary to the wish of the Court of Directors, aggressive wars and acts of spoliation were from time to time occurring in India, yet, on the other hand, both Wellesley and Ellenborough were called to such account as was within the power of that Court, and, at all events, there was an intelligent and experienced public body conspicuously connecting India with England.

Now that this is no longer the case, it becomes extremely important that England should most vigilantly watch, lest mischief should be done in her majestic name. To adopt a legal phrase, she must exercise an appellate jurisdiction; but the action of first instance must proceed upon the spot. India, like all other parts of the empire, has two sides—one imperial, the other local. To deal with the former and leave the latter alone, this is the brief enunciation of our problem, as far as the Home Government is concerned. Its solution is hinted at in many parts of the preceding pages. Take up your *Times* during the Session, and you will find the columns of debates headed "Imperial Parliament," yet that Parliament only represents the Lords and Commons of England, Scotland, Ireland, and a few smaller islands. If these really made up the empire, it would not be either very large or very great; but they do not.

I am not writing from a colonial point of view, but only as a person interested in the welfare of a conquered dependency, with certain colonial tendencies. In the former case, it would be my duty to show how the want of colonial representation in the congress of the empire weakens the cement of the whole fabric; how it leaves the colonies exposed to wars, in the proclaiming of which they have no voice; and entails upon England the expense and anxiety of defending them against dangers which she may have done nothing to provoke; lastly, how, by the absence of an imperial zollverein, it enables each colony to carry out an old-world system of customs, which may, and sometimes does, assume a character hostile to the best interests of the empire.

But in India few or none of these evils are to be apprehended. With the electric telegraph at hand, no viceroy can in future wage war on his own account, without imperial sanction, and no continental war that would be likely to affect India would be entered upon, in these days of non-intervention, without reference to the fact, that England is—to borrow Mr. Disraeli's epigram—an "Asiatic power." And the attempt made a few years ago to protect the native looms by putting on prohibitive duties on Manchester piece-goods was promptly put down and is not likely to be repeated.

But what guarantee have we against the fitful intermission of ignorant zeal amidst long pauses of deep neglect; that government by flashes of lightning, to which reference has already been made, and from which India has already suffered? I may have seemed in these pages to have said too little about the state and feelings of native society; but indeed that subject has never for a moment been absent from my thoughts while writing, because, to improve the administration of the country is surely the first and greatest boon that can be conferred upon the people; and all that I am urging must be regarded as means to that end.—Now the people of this country are cautious to a fault, and very seldom express an opinion until they have ascertained how it will be received. The following squib, therefore, from a native paper, deserves the more notice:—

"*Article I.*—In two years' time, lands, assigned for the revenue of temples and mosques (not churches) will be confiscated. *Article II.*—Any newspaper writer convicted of writing against the Christian religion, will be punished by a fine of rs. 1,000, and two years' imprisonment with hard labour. *Article III.*—All women, of whatever creed, will be forcibly remarried after the death of their husbands, even a third time if necessary, under penalty of a fine of rs. 1,000, with five years' imprisonment." —(*From the "Nasim Jounpooree," quoted in Report on the Native Press published by Government, N. W. P.*, 1866.)

The article from which the extract is taken is of the nature of those which appear in comic periodicals at home, and purports, playfully, to be an order by Queen Victoria; but when such jokes are current among the natives, a pretty fair index is afforded of the direction of their thoughts. Nor is there anything so very *outré* in the humour of the writer. Exeter Hall is a strong interest in England still; and a wave of fanaticism sweeping over the constituencies might land upon our shores some such ill-omened drift, not to be removed until it had executed its errand of mistrust and hatred. Suppose the various missionary bodies, forgetful of the true spirit of their holy Master, were to execute a combined attack upon the India Office during the temporary incumbency of some nobleman of Lord Shaftesbury's school; it is surely not impossible, in the present state of things, that a despatch might be sent out diverting to the Christian propaganda some portion of the revenues of India. Left to himself, no viceroy, whatever his convictions as a man, would venture upon a measure which he knows would lay the train of an explosion to which 1857 would be mere pyrotechnics.

I may have views of my own upon the reasons which retard the spread of Christianity in this country; but this is not the place to discuss them, nor have they the least bearing upon the present question. All honour to the good and earnest men who come amongst a sly and selfish people of idol-worshippers, where no social bonds are acknowledged but those of the family and the tribe, proclaiming the claims of humanity, the victory of suffering, the "great gain" of godly self-sacrifice, the universal fatherhood of the Maker of mankind. But they know who it was that said, that His kingdom was not of this world; and they should be the last to wish to see the hand of the King stretched forth towards the ark of God.

To myself the remedy appears to involve a reversal of that part of the recent policy which deprives the Indian councillors of seats in parliament. For instance, when Sir John Lawrence retires from the viceroyship, he will most probably be rewarded with an English peerage. In that case, he will be *ex vi naturali* excluded from the India Office! I do not know what minor advantages would be compensation for such a loss. The object sought by the measure was, I believe, the securing of the autocracy of one cabinet minister responsible to parliament and the country, but not fettered by the public opposition of his advisers. But my review has, I hope, shown that this object, as far as it has been gained, has not been beneficial; and that for all, or nearly all, the good that India has ever derived from England, she is indebted to the Directors, who were admitted to the House of Commons like any other men, and had not to choose between the surrender of a connection with the country they knew best, and an abnegation of the proudest privilege of an English citizen.

It is not for me, the denizen of a distant dependency, to speculate upon constitutional matters in the mother-country. I have pointed out our wants, it is for others to provide for their redress. If some scheme of nominee Indian members of the House of Commons, or the House of Lords, could be devised, which would not affect the balance of parties, a standing committee of parliament might be formed, in which Indian affairs might be discussed, and whose members might have a voice in the national council. Still more to the purpose would be an imperial congress, in which all colonies should be represented, and India also, as far as she has any colonial character, and whose province it should be to deal with those matters, and with those alone, which concerned the welfare of the empire at large, or of any portion of the empire in reference to imperial interests. Thus would England enter upon a long lease of renewed loyalty, in which the queen's name should still be a tower of strength, attracting eyes from all quarters of the globe, and proudly reminding every subject of an empire on which the sun never sets, that he, too, was one of its constituents, a citizen of no mean city. But this is a flight beyond my scope, which is only to impress upon true friends of India the necessity of disengaging her local administration, and obtaining for the local Government a controlled independence on those matters, and those alone, which are of local concernment.

At present this is far from being the case, and a general discontent is the natural result. The military have scarcely yet recovered from the soreness produced by years of ill-treatment; the civilians are alarmed about their pay, and discontented with their leave and pension rules; the merchants and planters dissatisfied with the tariff and the landed tenures, with their exclusion from all voice in domestic administration, and with the backwardness of public works, inseparable from the high rates of interest forced upon the Indian Government by the withholding of the imperial guarantee; the native princes trembling for their position; and the general native public looking forward sulkily to the imposition of a new income tax, or the propagation of Christianity by the State. No wonder if the magic influence of royal patronage has waned, and the tide of loyalty begun to turn. The vessel of State still floats, though the current is strong and treacherous, and the winds wild and wayward; but it is not the august name upon the taffrail, nor yet the bright blazon upon the bunting, that will keep her from wreck. The patriot who has shared her late dangers, and would speed her present voyage, will still feel the truth of the words of the Roman poet:—

> "Nil pictis timidus navita puppibus
>   Fidit; Tu nisi ventis
> Debes ludibrium, cave.
>
> Nuper solicitum quœ mihi tœdium,
> Nunc desiderium, curaque non levis,
>   Interfusa nitentes
>   Vites æquora Cycladas."

Whatever sky is above us, let us keep up our hearts; but they are still aching from the terrors of the last storm, and only long for calm. Let us have our sailing orders, and then let us navigate for ourselves, under the stars of heaven, not, like helpless passengers, battened down below whenever it blows, but trusted, each to do his duty in his appointed sphere, subject to no dictation but that of our experienced captain and his officers.

APPENDIX I.

[The following remarks, written on the spot during the first shock of the outbreak, describe the feeling with which it was then regarded.]

I venture to think that misapprehension as to the religious character of the Hindoostanees is very general. The Hindoo is ceremonious and pedantic in daily life, and the Mussulman often a fanatic when roused; but these creeds do not seem to have much positive or characteristic effect on the conduct or moral character of their respective professors. The moral and social habits of both classes are very similar. Caste, it is true, has a strong influence, so strong as to have embraced in its peculiar convolutions the descendants of the conquering race; the Mahomedans of India being quite as tenacious of its rules as their heathen brethren. But I do not look upon these obligations so much in the light of religious as social ties; for

I find that an argument on the subject always ends in bringing a native of this country to show that it is a mere matter of money. Thus when European ladies engage a wet-nurse, she at once undertakes to eat every description of European food, drink bottled ale, &c.; but she has along with her wages a sum of money, usually rs. 50, which is to purchase her re-instatement when discharged from her engagement.

The system can, in fact, be illustrated by supposing a gentleman in London to be "cut" by his society for some trivial offence, (say giving his guests bad wine,) and only re-admitted on asking all the leaders of *ton* to a *fête champêtre* of ruinous profusion.

But there is one religion warmly followed, and by all classes of the inhabitants, in this country—I mean the worship of "the Almighty Dollar" (or its better-half, the rupee). A sepoy, under the iron sway of military discipline, feels that his superiors might at any time easily insist on some rule which would clash against one of the many arbitrary ones of caste; and he would have the expense thrown on him of paying the necessary fees on being re-admitted. Hence, probably, the public have a dread of "attacks on the religion of the Sepoy" not found in Civil life. The Missionaries in this part of India make the reading of the Scriptures a *sine quâ non* for the pupils in their schools of whatever creed; but the education they offer is good, and their schools fill as well, and with boys of the same classes as those kept by Government, from which the Bible is banished. Again, the religion of the Sepoy (I mean his pocket) has been attacked in another way,—lately stringent rules having been issued for the guidance of invaliding committees, the effect of which is that no man can get his pension, (for however great a period he may have served,) so long as he is capable of standing up under his arms. This relieved the pension establishment; but has the play been worth the lights? It is the best of all securities for the allegiance of a mercenary army, and has an excellent effect on the popularity of a Government surely,—that the veteran soldier should retire with his medal, and his pension, and grow fat and old under his own fig-tree, singing in the ears of his fellow-villagers the praises of his liberal masters. But suppose the case of a man who cannot stand up with a sword on, his cheeks glued to his gums, his chin to his chest, and his paunch to his back-bone, with one foot in the grave, and the other in a bandage, and figure to yourself the encouraging prospect his lees of life will afford to those who may be thinking of entering the service. The exigencies of a country where taxation is unknown, and thought to be impossible, and where the most gigantic public works are imperatively insisted on by the people of England, thousands of miles off, naturally cause retrenchment to be considered the greatest of all reforms. To give an illustration. In Lord Dalhousie's reign it was found that we were at peace, but keeping up a war establishment of Commissariat carriage, camels, elephants, &c. This it was determined to put down, and leave armies to make their own arrangements, *pro re nata*, for hiring carriage when ordered on service. This reform saved, perhaps, rs. 70,000 a year, and when Delhi was attacked and conquered by the mutineers, it took the head-quarters of the army exactly a month to relieve it, from a distance of not 150 miles. All sorts of financial *mirage* allure a Governor-General thirsting for pension and promotion. Provinces must be annexed because they *may* pay, and it would be a good thing if we could resume a portion of the pension secured to the royal family at Delhi. The same reasons justify us here that justified us at Lucknow—the profligacy of the Eastern Courts, offensive to our moral judgment, made the unwilling spoliators seem victims and martyrs to their own excessive purity. Now let us suppose that in our Empire we have —1st, a body of over-drilled, unprincipled foreign prætorians, shorn of pensions and privileges; 2nd, a starved military administration; 3rd, weakened confidence in our national probity,—the great chiefs learning the fear of losing wealth and power, either from their own experience or the example of others, and it will not be difficult to see that something like what has taken place might have been looked for.

Nor were these the only discontents; and our military system has faults which greatly weakened us. The men were in a high state of pipe-clay, but were *too much alike;* each corps presented not only an uniform appearance, but an identity of organisation; the same strata ran through the whole army, and the shock of a convulsion breaking out in one spot ran through the whole. The commanding officers had no free scope of action, no power over their men; centralisation had brought in its usual procrustean red-tapery, and its dead level of mediocrity. A regiment's appearance in peace was taken as a sign of its efficiency in war; the colonel was saved the trouble of thinking for himself by the minutest rules; the sentence of a regimental court-martial was never sure to be final under the facility of appeals; the younger officers,—too few for an English system, too many for irregular management,—were men who have been sometimes, (in a phrase that has been mistaken,) called "the refuse," but of whom it would be enough to say that they were mostly such as, having been disappointed in endeavouring to get on staff or civil employ, looked upon their regiment as a penal settlement, a lot to be borne with murmuring, and escaped from on opportunity; where the men were shunned, as though they were the implements of torture, and duty regarded as a hateful task to be hurried over, that time might be passed in "cramming" for examinations, or in dancing round great men and their wives in Himalayan watering-places. Let me not speak too sweepingly; I speak unfortunately of what is the rule, though subject to numerous exceptions. That it is not the fault of the officers themselves, is clear from the great efficiency of the more fortunate members of the same class who entered the staff, became magistrates, or officered the irregular corps. But it stands to reason, that that cannot be a good system which teaches a young man, on entering the army, to make it his great object to get out of it, and which leads him to look upon his regiment as a refuge for the destitute, or a positive punishment, (it was not unfrequently so employed by the Supreme Government,) which keeps many of the seniors away from military duties till they have put on a third nature, and then sends them back to their corps, which they are to manage without powers, and without experience.

The Native Army, in this state of discontent and demoralisation, would form a fit subject for the treasonable tampering of the friends of the dethroned King of Oudh, or the threatened family of Delhi. A day fixed for a rising, imperfectly concerted plans, action precipitated by unfortunate, not to say injudicious treatment, panic and procrastination; . . . . here is the probable history of the origin of the Mutiny.—(*Extract from a letter, dated 6th June*, 1857.)

APPENDIX II.

In the chapter on "Home" administration, a suggestion is made respecting the possibility of floating an issue of Exchequer Bills for small amounts bearing interest. If this could be done, it would certainly popularise the credit of Government, only it would be indispensable that the bills should be cashed, when due, at the Tréasury from which they were issued, at all events, if not elsewhere, and received at par in payment of Government demands. It is a curious fact, that the present writer did in 1857, when his was the only district in the north-west provinces that the disturbances had not reached, float such an issue, without Government sanction, (for which he was unable to apply owing to communication being cut off,) and this during the five months that the only British troops in the country were concentrated, 200 miles off, under the walls of Delhi.

When the time came, the Accountant of these provinces reported to Government that "the measures were highly successful, and he (the author) deserving of the thanks of Government. . . . . The fact of notes of any kind having been put and kept in circulation during the height of the Mutiny is very remarkable, and . . . . deserving of a place in history."* He also proposed that the notes should be continued, and a similar system of local divisional paper currencies extended to other stations, expressing his confidence of success. (It is hardly necessary to add that none of this was done.)

* Accountant, North-West Provinces, to Secretary to Government, dated Agra, 21st January, 1859.